# *Beyond O.J.*

Also by Earl Ofari Hutchinson

The Myth of Black Capitalism
Let Your Motto Be Resistance
The Mugging of Black America
Black Fatherhood: The Guide to Male Parenting
Black Fatherhood II: Black Women Talk About Their Men
The Assassination of the Black Male Image
Blacks and Reds: Race and Class in Conflict, 1919-1990

# Beyond *O.J.*

## Race, Sex, *a*nd Class Lessons *for* America

by Earl Ofari Hutchinson, Ph.D.

Montréal/New York
London

Black Rose Books No. Z236
Hardcover ISBN: 1-55164-051-1(bound)
Paperback ISBN: 1-55164-050-3 (pbk.)

**Canadian Cataloguing in Publication Data**

Ofari, Earl
Beyond O.J. : race, sex, and class lessons for America

Canadian ed.
Includes bibliographical references and index.
ISBN 1-55164-051-1 (bound) -
ISBN 1-55164-050-3 (pbk.)

1. United States—Race relations. 2. Racism—United States. 3. Afro-Americans—
Social conditions. 4. Interracial marriage. 5. Social classes—United States.
I. Title
HT1521.O33 1996     305.896'073     C96-900269-6

Cover design and illustration by Lighthourne Images © 1995


Mailing Address

BLACK ROSE BOOKS
C.P. 1258
Succ. Place du Parc
Montréal, Québec
H2W 2R3 Canada

BLACK ROSE BOOKS
340 Nagel Drive
Cheektowaga, New York
14225 USA


To order books:  (phone) 1-800-565-9523  (fax) 1-800-221-9985


*A publication of the Institute of Policy Alternatives of Montréal* (IPAM)
Printed in Canada

## Dedication

To those who realized that the real meaning of the O.J. saga lay outside, not inside the courtroom.

## Acknowledgment

The O.J. case was more than a tabloid obsession. It was a window of opportunity to discuss the issues that plague America. I give grateful thanks to Matt Blair, Rene Childress, Angela Collins, Joye Day, Madeleine Schwab, and especially my publisher Barbara Bramwell. Their comments, criticisms, and suggestions helped me clarify these issues.

# Table of Contents

## Introduction
# *Beyond O.J.*

*T*his is a book about O.J. Simpson—and much more. It has to be. Although I was a Simpson trial news analyst for the CBS-TV affiliate in Los Angeles, I did not know him personally. I met him only once and that was by chance. It was in the spring of 1969 at a fraternity party near the USC campus. O.J. was a senior. He had just won the Heisman Trophy and was everyone's All-American. He was practically a household name in Los Angeles and much of the nation.

The party was packed. The liquor was flowing. Everyone was dancing and having a good time. O.J., his first wife, Marquerite, and another man were sitting in a room adjacent to the kitchen, away from everyone. They were talking quietly. I paused for a moment in the kitchen and watched them. Party goers would saunter into the room to shake his hand and make small talk. Some asked for an autograph. I resisted as long as I could. Finally, I walked in, shook his hand, made small talk about football, and wished him well. O.J. was gracious and polite. He smiled and acknowledged the glad handers. He was not arrogant or condescending.

I could sense that he wanted to maintain his distance. O.J. was conscious of his image and status. There was a clear line of demarcation between him and the public. He existed in a world that few could ever enter. O.J. was a superstar, an all-American hero athlete. He was a man consigned to a life of splendid isolation.

The O.J. case generated an estimated gross domestic product of $200 million. This was bigger than the GDP of some Caribbean nations. A legion of TV talking heads, legal experts, and opinion news commentators made money and furthered their careers theorizing, gossiping, and speculating about O.J. and the murders of Nicole Brown Simpson and Ronald Goldman. Much of the American public also spent endless hours theorizing, gossiping, and speculating about O.J. and the murders. The media and the public reminded me of the people at the party. Like me, they talked about a man they could never really know. The three persons who knew O.J. best were: Marquerite; his mother, Eunice Simpson; and his football pal and confidant, Al Cowlings. They either refused to talk or gave guarded interviews to the media about him.

Still the press nearly killed the goose that laid the golden egg. The instant the murders of Nicole Simpson and Ronald Goldman were made public, the media dumped onto the public an unprecedented avalanche of tabloid-style rumors, innuendo, gossip, and lies about O.J. The TV networks announced plans to air quickie kiss-and-tell soap dramas purportedly based on his life. Much of the public got sick of it. It soon became common to hear people say, "Oh God, I don't want to hear or read anything else about O.J."

There will be no explosive exposes, revelations, or true confessions about O.J., Nicole, or the murders in this book. I am not interested in titillating or tantalizing anyone with stories of domestic violence, lesbian affairs, sex orgies, cocaine parties, Mafia hit men, or secret confessions. I am not going to speculate about whether someone else did it or why.

I will not second guess the defense, the prosecution, or analyze legal strategy, coroner's errors, crime scene contamination, the reliability of DNA, Johnnie Cochran's attire, Marcia Clark's hairstyles, or how many times the bailiffs searched O.J.'s suits before he changed to come into and leave the courtroom. I was not concerned with that during the months the O.J. case dominated the conversations at dinner tables in America. I am not concerned with it now. Before the trial, as far as the public knew, the only people who really knew who committed the murders were the killer(s).

This didn't stop others from turning wild speculation into fast cash. Three instant "life of O.J. books" were on newsstands and in bookstores within days after his arrest. Another gossipy, trash-toned book on O.J. and Nicole released the same week as Pope John's best-seller, *Crossing the Threshold of Hope*, racked up one-third more sales that week.

More books will be published about his life, the murders, and his legal battles in the years to come. The O.J. case spawned a new grossly prurient literary genre. But I'm not concerned with that.

What I am concerned with is that the O.J. case made America realize:

- Interracial sex and marriage is the last taboo for whites and blacks.
- There is a slavish need to make icons of its celebrities and sports heroes.
- Many Americans relentlessly manufacture racial, sexual, and class stereotypes and scapegoats.
- There is a retreat into dangerous political know-nothingness in America.
- Many blacks have been driven to the unshakable belief that there are secret plots, conspiracies, and hidden plans to eliminate them.
- Much of the media has turned into gossip and titillation tabloids.
- Many blacks and whites play the race card.
- Justice is peddled to the highest bidder.

This book will tell why these issues go beyond O.J.

## one
# Interracial Sex and Marriage: The Last Taboo

*"Did you try to keep that Negro from Miss Dalton? Answer yes or no!"*

*"Have you a sister?"*

*"Is she married?"*

*"Would you consent for her to marry a Negro?"*

$T$he moment murder charges were filed against O.J. I re-read that passage from Richard Wright's novel, *Native Son*. The parallel between O.J.'s plight and that of Wright's principal character Bigger Thomas, a black male, seemed disturbingly real. Thomas became the object of a furious manhunt, intense media hysteria, and a racially-charged trial. Thomas had committed a heinous crime. He had murdered Mary Dalton, a white woman. But as the angry attack by the prosecutor on Dalton's Communist-leaning, white boyfriend (fiancee) suggested, Bigger wasn't solely being tried for murder.

The prosecutor and the public suspected that Bigger had an illicit sexual relationship with her; privately he was being judged for that too. This was America's ultimate taboo. It didn't matter that he had never had sexual relations with Mary Dalton. The mere thought that he did was enough to seal his doom. Bigger was convicted and executed.

Bigger Thomas became a powerful symbol for much of American society's fear, hatred of, and rage against sexual relations between black men and white women. The pictures of O.J. and Nicole Simpson together that appeared on the covers of nearly every national magazine the week after his arrest made me think of Bigger. Would this be a chilling reminder to many whites that a black man, albeit a wealthy and famous one, had violated America's last taboo against interracial sex? Would this reinforce the persistent fear many whites (and some blacks) have of black men as hypersexual and dangerous?

This was not paranoia or false fear. In the *Newsweek* cover story of its August 22, 1994 issue entitled "The Double Life of O.J. Simpson" *Newsweek* neatly cropped an inside photo that showed two persons. One was a bikini clad white woman in a sexually suggestive pose. The other was O.J. supposedly leering at her. The caption read: "duty and obsession." O.J.'s alleged obsession was his "lust after only white women." *Newsweek* also tossed in a jibe from his first wife, Marguerite. She reportedly called him a "beast."

The picture was taken at a combined birthday and graduation party for O.J. and his daughter, Arnelle. The woman was a comic stripper hired by friends as a party joke. Dozens of people saw her act at O.J. and Arnelle's party and laughed. But O.J. was the only one shown. He protested: "The photographer who took that picture knows the truth and *Newsweek* had a responsibility to report the truth." O.J. was right. It was unpardonable media muckraking designed solely to titillate. But O.J. was also naive.

The truth is the picture worked. *Newsweek* successfully pushed America's oldest hot button: Black man+lust+white woman+scorned black woman=sexual brute. O.J. became an instant metaphor and warning to America of the menace posed by the abusive and sexually plundering black male. The myth has stirred deep fantasies and fear within much of American society. It is a part of America's sordid and shameful history of racial and sexual stereotyping that has refused to die.

In 1994, writer Michael Ortiz studied the dream content of more than one hundred white persons. There was one constant horror in their dreams: "It is the black man's phallus, knife, gun, public anger—or the stealth with which he climbs into the window at night—that most frightens white people."

These fears still persist among many Americans. The media scrupulously avoided making overt racial references to O.J. and Nicole's marriage. There was no need. The pictures of the couple were, in themselves, enough of an explicit reference.

But, many Americans looked at their marriage in different ways. Some were indifferent. Others regarded it as a sign that America had junked the taboo and attached no particular significance to the marriage of a black man to a white woman.

Some simply saw O.J. as an exceptionally successful black man and a glamorous celebrity with mainstream cross-over appeal who posed no racial threat. To them their marriage made sense.

That was wishful thinking. Simpson was not an exception. The taboo against interracial sex has never completely died. It is too solidly rooted in the complex mix of racial and sexual fears that still define relations between black men and white women, and white men and black women. Many white men still believe that all black men are obsessed with having sexual relations with white women. Many blacks believe the same thing. If one black man such as O.J. marries or has relations with a white woman, he represents black men universally. This belief is irrational, absurd, and deadly real.

• • • • • •

*T*he taboo against sex and marriage between black men and white women has a long history that has been nearly impossible to shed thanks in part to the federal government. Early on, it decided to intrude into the bedrooms of America. The Supreme Court in 1883 upheld an Alabama law that made it a felony crime for black men and white women to have sex, while sex between white men and black women was tacitly accepted.

The Court brushed aside objections that the law violated the equal protection clause of the Fourteenth Amendment since blacks and whites (women that is) were supposedly prosecuted equally. This bizarre logic held. For the next century, interracial sex and marriage in America would not be a crime in the South, but a national crime. The fear of black men making love to white women would be the X factor that instantly stirred latent racial hatreds and touched off mob violence.

An athlete even more celebrated than O.J. in his day found that out the hard way. Heavyweight champion Jack Johnson had wealth, world-wide fame, and the adulation of the sports world. Even though it was the era of lynchings and legal segregation, Johnson, like O.J., still managed to win the admiration of many whites for his sports prowess. This did not protect him from legal attacks.

In November 1912, the federal government accused him of violating the Mann Act for traveling across state lines with his white mistress. The law, passed in 1910 and formally known as the White Slave Traffic Act, was the brainchild of the prudish and taciturn Republican Congressman, James Robert Mann.

It was partly a product of the pseudo-moral hypocrisy of post-Victorian America, and partly a reaction to public fear that hordes of foreign women were being smuggled into America for prostitution. Ninety-eight percent of the convictions under the Mann Act in the first two years were for the operation of brothels, dens, and organized sex rings with white women as prostitutes or merely consorting participants.

The law was not explicitly aimed at blacks or Johnson. Attorney General George Wickersham did not intend to use it for political harassment. When Johnson thumbed his nose at

America's moral pretensions and publicly flaunted his white women, the public and Wickersham were happy to make him an exception, and thereby, an example.

"Bad Nigger" Johnson compounded the "crime" when he made Lucille Cameron, a white teenager, his second wife. Blacks were traumatized. The headline in the black weekly, *The Philadelphia Tribune* screamed, "JACK JOHNSON DANGEROUSLY ILL, VICTIM OF WHITE FEVER." The Reverend Adam Clayton Powell, Sr. knew that the white response would be swift and savage. He vainly pled with Americans not to hold black men responsible for "the actions of a single member." It did.

At the Annual Governors Conference in December 1912, the governors of New Jersey, New York, Pennsylvania, Ohio, and Connecticut were in hot competition to be the first on record to support bills to outlaw interracial marriage. A week later Georgia Democrat Seaborn A. Roddenberg turned up the heat. He introduced a congressional amendment to impose a federal ban on interracial marriages stating: "Interracial marriage between whites and blacks is repulsive and averse to every sentiment of the pure American spirit."

Roddenberg soon had much of America whistling Dixie. Within weeks there were twenty-one similar bills pending in Congress. In racially-polarized pre-World War I America, Johnson symbolized all black men. Thousands of black waiters, porters, barbers, and laborers were fired.

Legislators in Wisconsin, Iowa, Kansas, Colorado, Minnesota, and Michigan didn't wait for their governors to take action. They rapidly passed laws that outlawed interracial marriage. Some were worried that the mob hysteria could get out of hand and touch off a destructive race war nationally. The *New York Times* and a scattering of other Northern newspapers urged moderation.

The few stray editorials published in Northern papers condemning violence meant little in the South. White Southerners relied on the standard method: intimidation and terror. The law became a harsh tool of racial repression and a thinly disguised cover for sexual revenge against black men.

O.J. never mentioned Johnson by name, but he strongly hinted that in part he believed that he was being persecuted for his marriage to Nicole. O.J. was guilty of hyperbole. There was no comparison between the near lynch mob atmosphere that dogged Johnson nearly a century ago and his case. Yet O.J. understood that sex and race were volatile issues that could raise the passions of many people particularly when a black man was accused of a crime against a white woman. In those instances guilt or innocence was not the issue. The word of the white female accuser, particularly in the South, was the issue and the law.

• • • • • •

*I*t isn't necessary to reach back to the sordid history of lynching to confirm that black men have been sexually typecast. Present day events offer enough proof. The *Dallas Herald* reviewed all felony cases in the county for 1988 and found that when a black male was charged with the rape of a white woman the average sentence was ten years. When a black woman was the victim, the average sentence was two years. Black men charged with crimes against whites, particularly white women, receive stiffer sentences than crimes against black women.

Even when they don't commit crimes, black men may still be at risk with the law. In Bakersfield, 100 miles north of the courtroom where O.J. was tried, Charles Tomlin had three strikes against him in 1978. He was accused of killing a white drug dealer. The witness was a white woman. The police knew that Tomlin dated (and married) a white woman. There was no other solid evidence that he was guilty, and plenty that he wasn't.

He was tried and sentenced to a term of twenty-five years to life. Seventeen years later the witness recanted her testimony. His attorney admitted his defense was incompetent and witnesses swore that the police had vowed to get Tomlin because of his association with a white woman. The police refused to confirm or deny this to reporters.

What if Tomlin hadn't found a maverick attorney who believed in his innocence? What if the woman hadn't agreed to tell the truth? What if the court had simply denied his appeal? If any of these "what ifs" hadn't happened, he would have rotted in prison probably for the rest of his life. As it turned out the criminal justice system forced Tomlin to waste the best years of his youth in prison, not because he committed a crime but because he fit a stereotype.

O.J. was bothered by the Tomlin case. He viewed it as a gross example of justice gone badly awry. More likely he saw a little bit of himself in Tomlin. If Tomlin could be framed and railroaded to prison for crimes he didn't commit, then O.J. believed he could, too. But there was a difference. Tomlin was young, poor, and black; and from all indications, a convenient patsy of a flawed justice system. His story is not uncommon. O.J. was middle-aged, self-assured, and privileged. He could hardly be called a weak and compliant victim of corrupt and bigoted police and city officials, even if he thought he was. The fact that there was an arguably similar perverse overtone of racial and sexual bias in his case and Tomlin's was reason to be troubled. At least O.J. was.

• • • • • •

While polls show that the majority of white Americans no longer oppose interracial marriages, many still do. A 1991 poll by the National Opinion Research Center of 1,500 Americans found that one in five white Americans believed interracial marriage should be illegal. They frowned on marriage between black men and white women the most. Sixty-six percent opposed a close relative marrying a black man. Only forty-five percent were opposed to marriage with a Latino or Asian and fifteen percent to a Jew.

During the years that he was married to Nicole, O.J.'s name and celebrity status partially shielded him from the resentment often reserved for black men and white women who marry. There is no record during this time that O.J. acknowledged society's less than enlightened attitude on interracial marriage or that he ever complained of harassment.

Following his arrest and jailing, he publicly admitted that maybe he and Nicole lived a fairy tale existence. He charged that some white Americans were using him "as an example" to warn white women away from having relationships with black men. O.J. was convinced that the jurors thought the same way. He didn't say how he could know that the jurors were overtly hostile to him for marrying Nicole. The real point was that he felt that he was judged, and condemned by some, for breaking society's unstated prohibition against interracial relationships.

South African expatriate Mark Mathabane, whose wife is white, recounts in his book, *Love in Black and White,* their nasty encounters with racism in both the North and the South. They did not face lynch mobs nor were they driven from neighborhoods.

The hostile stares, insults, harassment, and indifference they experienced from strangers, some friends, and even relatives reminded them that many still regarded black men married to white women as social pariahs. This is why black and white marriages are a rarity. According to the 1990 Census, only four percent of black men marry white women. There is yet another reason why.

• • • • • •

*I*mmediately after O.J.'s arrest, former Nation of Islam national spokesman Khalid Muhammad claimed that O.J. was in trouble because he was "sleeping with the enemy." The "enemy" was Nicole Brown Simpson. To Muhammad she was not simply O.J.'s ex-wife. She was his *white* ex-wife. It was tempting to dismiss the remark as the overblown raving of a black rabble-rouser. But Muhammad only said what many blacks thought. While a majority of African-Americans for much of the trial didn't believe that O.J. murdered Nicole and Goldman, many did think he committed racial treason by marrying her.

The O.J. and Nicole tragedy pricked a malignant sore among many blacks, particularly black women. While many publicly supported O.J. and argued that he was innocent before and during the trial, privately they accused him of having an incurable "jungle fever" obsession with Nicole. Some believed that he had courted danger by marrying Nicole. It was a rough sentiment but the anger was genuine.

Many black women were hurt that O.J. shared his elegant lifestyle with Nicole. The glitter couple lived in a five million dollar Brentwood estate, vacationed in a $1.9 million Laguna Beach condo and an expensive San Francisco condo, and maintained an "exclusive" apartment in New York. There were private jets to whisk them to weekend resorts in Hawaii, Aspen, Mexico, and gambling junkets to Las Vegas.

There were visits to expensive tanning salons, gyms, dance clubs, expensive therapists, and bi-weekly nutritional consultants. Nicole was never short of cash when she went out on the town. She was allotted $6,000 a month in pocket money. To keep her wardrobe up to date, she annually spent upwards of $48,000 on clothing.

After their marital split in July 1992, Nicole wasn't reduced to sackcloth and ashes. She received a generous property and cash settlement. A grateful Nicole admitted, "The lifestyle that O.J. and I shared was truly substantial." She lived a rich and famous lifestyle of which most black women could only dream.

To many black women, O.J. was another sad example of a prominent black man rejecting his own community and especially its women. He was the most famous symbol and target of black female frustration with black men marrying white women.

• • • • • •

Many blacks have long resented interracial marriages. Before the Supreme Court in 1967 struck down all state bans against interracial marriage, surveys showed that almost as many blacks as whites frowned on black and white marriages. The ambivalence remains. A National Opinion Research Center poll in 1991 found that two-thirds of blacks neither "favored nor opposed" interracial marriage. Although anti-miscegenation laws were brutal racial exclusionary measures designed to reinforce black inferiority, the poll revealed that nearly one in ten blacks still thought interracial marriages should be illegal.

Three years later little had changed: forty percent of black women and a significant percentage of black men said they would not date a person of another race. Gail Mathabane, in *Love in Black and White,* discovered that the attitudes of many blacks on interracial marriage were still petrified. For a moment, when she accompanied her husband, Mark, to an interview at an all-black radio station, she thought she was in Antarctica. The stares from some staff members were icy. "I realized that I was regarded as 'the white woman' who stole a black man." Their hateful stares consigned her to a netherworld that was impossible to escape. "I felt like I had committed some unspoken crime."

Many black women and men who oppose interracial marriage are convinced that black men are mesmerized by European beauty standards and regard white women as trophies that fulfill their desire for power, status, and acceptance in the white-dominated world. They are nagged by the thought that black men see them as poor imitations of white women.

Eldridge Cleaver, in *Soul on Ice,* confirmed their worst fears. He called the white woman the "reincarnation of the Virgin Mary." He seemed proud of his sexual conquests, even rapes of white women. If Cleaver specialized in, and gloated over, raping white women, he was the rare exception. Black men don't routinely rape white women. Nor do white men routinely rape black women. Rape, like most crime in America, is intra-racial. It's black-on-black, white-on-white, Latino-on-Latino, and Asian-on-Asian. In many cases, the rape victim knows her assailant.

Self-confirmed rapist Cleaver was widely quoted and held

up by many, who should have known better, as the voice of authority on black male/white female relations. He confidently asserted that "if a white leader wanted to unite blacks, offer every black man a white woman."

This kind of base sensationalism made him famous and his book a best-seller. It also fed the dangerous myth that black men would abandon wives, lovers, children, relatives, and their community in a shameless and never-ending carnal hunt for white flesh. Neither Cleaver, nor his admirers were much on facts. In 1967, when his book was published, more than nine out of ten black men married black women, including Cleaver. His wife, Kathleen, was black. More than a quarter century later, the percentage rate for black male-female marriages was virtually the same.

O.J. was vilified by many blacks for his obsessive pursuit of white women. They conveniently forgot that he was married to a black woman, Marguerite, for twelve years. He maintained the marriage even during the years he was a football superstar and media celebrity. There is no evidence that O.J. abandoned Marguerite to chase Nicole. In fact, Marguerite hinted that it might have been the other way around. She in part blamed Nicole for breaking up their marriage. She claimed Nicole incessantly called and tried to visit O.J.

Still, an element of Cleaver's tortured and convoluted logic made good sense to those who stubbornly believe that a white woman spells F-R-E-E-D-O-M and E-S-C-A-P-E for black men. It was a variation on the old notion that a black man who dates or marries a white woman has a terminal identity crisis as a result of low self-esteem and is using her to escape from his own characteristic "blackness." He is the prototypic marginal man rejected by a hostile white world and seeking escape from an insecure and fearful black world. This alleged self-hate-filled black man can never belong to either. There is no end to the reasons given to explain the aberrant sexual behavior of a black man and a white woman who mate. They are:

- Rebelling against authority;
- Repudiating society's norms and values;
- Answering the call of the jungle; and
- Infatuated with the sexual exotica of each other.

Much of this boils down to opinion, gossip, anecdote, rumor, envy, jealousy, and ignorance. There is no evidence that black men and white women who date or marry are psychologically impaired. The degree of personal and professional compatibility between them often matches or exceeds that of black couples.

The separation/divorce rate for black male/white female couples is only marginally less than black couples. Black and white marriages generally last as long as and are as stable as the marriages of couples of the same race. Mixed couples have to have stronger personalities, character, and more self-assurance to withstand the stares, harassment, and hostility from many blacks and whites.

Many blacks repeated the standard stereotypical reasons to explain why O.J. supposedly insanely pursued white women and married Nicole. Los Angeles County Deputy District Attorney Christopher A. Darden, a lead prosecutor in the case, fell into the same silly trap. He slyly hinted in open court that O.J. had a "fetish" for "blond-haired white women." O.J.'s critics claimed to either have known him personally or to have had insider's knowledge of his love affairs. They didn't, but it made for good gossip.

O.J. and Nicole probably heard all of the accusations, gossip, and innuendoes about them during the years they were married. He complained about blacks who attacked him for saying "you shouldn't go out with a white woman." O.J. took pains to assure that he loved and married Nicole because of common interests and shared experiences. He was being honest. If Nicole had been a gold digging groupie or career wife, she would not have signed away all claims to his estimated $10 million estate *before* their marriage. Their relationship and marriage couldn't have lasted a decade-and-half if it had been based on lust or infatuation.

• • • • • •

*M*any blacks have contracted a near terminal case of tunnel vision to facts like this. And as more black men became wealthy and famous in politics, business, sports, and entertainment, the grumbles of some have increased. More black women charged that many of them considered only white women as worthy mates. And that white women were "using" these men to elevate their own socioeconomic status.

During the Clarence Thomas Supreme Court confirmation hearings, I remember one black woman angrily muttering,

"Why is *she* sitting behind him." The *she* was Ginni Thomas, Clarence's white wife, who daily accompanied him to the hearings. Thomas's wife was a professional, from a solid middle-class family.

But to many blacks, the Thomas's were another example of a prominent black man choosing a lower-class white woman when there were countless talented and educated black women professionals who could have matched him in income and education. Their cathartic anger reflected the pain and rejection they felt that a black woman wasn't sitting there *and* the mistaken belief that black men habitually choose lower-status white women as mates.

The opposite is usually the case. Thomas's wife was not an exception. The white women that date and marry black men generally match their partner in income, education, and social outlook. Education is the strongest determinant of marriage success. Black women with the same educational level as their husbands were the strongest survivors. If white women have the same educational level as their black mates, their marriage is only marginally less likely to survive.

The fear of prominent, educated black men en masse marrying white women is a false fear. It may have been fashionable to brand O.J. or Clarence Thomas racial traitors. But celebrities such as Magic Johnson, Michael Jordan, Muhammad Ali, George Foreman, Eddie Murphy, Bill Cosby, Denzel Washington, Spike Lee, Jesse Jackson, Andrew Young, and John H. Johnson as well as many other athletes, entertainers, and prominent professionals married black women.

Some of the black men that do marry white women, and there are more numerically than a decade ago, may be motivated by sexual idolatry, but most aren't. They have more opportunities to meet and interact with whites at colleges, in the workplace, and in social settings. In the coming years, more black men will marry white women (and black women will marry white men). They will still be a distinct minority.

This is what angered many blacks about O.J. and Nicole. They believed that he was the eternal symbol of the successful black man who loses his racial moorings and commits sexual treason by marrying white. Many whites believed that his fame as an athlete, entertainer, and media personality earned him mainstream acceptance, hero status, and an exemption from racial backlash for marrying Nicole. Both were mistaken. O.J. did not commit racial or sexual treason by marrying Nicole. Nor did he gain a full exemption from racial and sexual stereotyping.

Black men and white women in intimate relationships have inflamed passions, stirred fears, and ignited violence for decades. The Supreme Court lifted the ban on miscegenation, but it did not totally change public attitudes. Interracial marriage remains the last taboo. In time that will change. Love and marriage can't be regulated by an artificial standard of emotional or racial correctness.

O.J. stood trial for murder, not for "sleeping with the enemy" or violating the last taboo.

## two
# *America's Poster Boy for Sexual Deviancy*

*O*.J.'s face nearly jumped off the poster the young woman carried. The caption read: "Are you a victim of domestic violence?" The phone number underneath was that of the San Diego police department. Police departments in other cities duplicated and widely circulated the poster as flyers. Women were urged to immediately report any physical abuse to the police.

A month after O.J.'s arrest, I appeared on the *Rolanda* show with two other male panelists to discuss racism and the O.J. Simpson case. During the question period, a young woman stood up. She shook with rage as she reminded us that O.J. battered Nicole. The young woman described the emotional trauma she too had suffered after a sexual assault.

To her, O.J. was not a man accused of murder. He was not a victim of a racially biased criminal justice system. He was a wife batterer. The issue was domestic violence, not race.

Thousands of women agreed with her.

O.J. propelled the issue of spousal abuse and domestic violence from bedroom privacy to public outrage. The case had all the ingredients of high camp drama: a superstar celebrity, a well-publicized case of domestic abuse, leaked 911 tapes, a handslap sentence, and finally a double murder. The culprit was black; a convicted batterer and the accused murderer of his white ex-wife.

Prosecutors contended that O.J.'s rage, jealousy, and violence against Nicole drove him to kill when he could no longer "control her." They had a smoking gun: O.J.'s contrite letter to Nicole apologizing "for hurting you."

The defense was right on one point. Even if O.J. was guilty of assaulting Nicole, it did not mean he was guilty of murdering her. Most husbands that batter their wives don't kill them. There is also some support for this in law. Convicting someone on the basis of committing prior bad acts violates the concept of legal fairness. Los Angeles County Deputy District Attorney Marcia Clark bulled ahead anyway.

When defense attorneys learned that a Latina juror had allegedly been beaten by her boyfriend, they demanded that she be removed. Clark dug in. This was just the kind of juror she wanted. She argued that the juror could be objective toward Simpson since the juror had no physical scars from the alleged beating. With no trace of shamefacedness, Clark even told the judge that the woman "did not consider pushing and shoving to be physical abuse." Clark's tortured no harm no foul redefinition of domestic violence went nowhere. The juror was dismissed.

Clark was still optimistic. The majority of the jurors were female and African-American. Two of them had experienced domestic abuse. Clark gambled that they would instantly buy the prosecution's shaky argument that domestic violence leads to murder.

There were two problems. Polls consistently showed that black women by far bigger percentages than even black men publicly said that O.J. was innocent. Her own jury consultants warned that much more research was needed to support the assumption that women would automatically connect domestic violence to murder.

They were right. Dismissed jurors later said that the prosecution did not make a convincing case that O.J.'s prior physical assault against Nicole led directly to her murder. One dismissed juror, Jeanette Harris, went even further. She was livid at the prosecutors for "casting me in the light of being a victim" of domestic violence. She made the rounds of nearly every TV talk show "to clear the air" that she had not been abused by her husband. This was a damaging blow to the prosecution's badly crafted theory. Prosecutors listened and tactfully backed away. They decided not to call additional witnesses to discuss domestic violence.

The defense was wrong on another point. Feminist groups and their critics tossed out wildly disparate figures on the number of women battered annually—from 4 million down to 100,000—to prove or disprove that it was a crisis issue. But many women were being hurt in their homes. In 1992, the

Surgeon General confirmed that a major cause of injury to women in America was domestic battering.

Since the mid-1980's, 1,500 women have been murdered yearly by their husbands, boyfriends, or lovers. Wives that are murdered are almost always killed by their husbands and there is generally a history and pattern of domestic assault that precedes the murder. In this case, Nicole was dead. And O.J was the only suspect.

This touched off a national storm. The hot line phones at women's shelters and centers jumped off the hook. In New York, the calls leaped twenty-seven percent; thirty-five percent in Denver; eighty percent in Houston; and eighty percent in Los Angeles. There were even self-confessionals by batterers. One said, "I don't want it to turn into what happened with O.J." Many media analysts enthusiastically predicted that the O.J. case would publicize the crime of spousal abuse. They were right.

The media, which previously had turned a deaf ear to the pleas of women's rights advocates to publicize domestic violence abuses, were in a frenzy. They deluged the public with angry and hypocritical editorials, exposes, features, and TV reports that expressed moral outrage. The politicians, equally mute on the issue in the past, were glued to the *Oprah* and *Donahue* shows. They sniffed the changing air of public mood and rushed into action. Legislators in dozens of states rushed through laws that authorized arrests and toughened penalties against domestic violence.

Congress, occasionally alert to the changing trends and to

the approaching 1994 mid-year elections, expressed indignation. Women legislators vowed to pull the Violence Against Women Act out of congressional mothballs and secure passage. The law would make violence against women a violation of civil rights, carrying civil and criminal penalties. The political candidates spotted political paydirt in the issue. Some even stepped over the line.

An openly lesbian Democratic state assembly candidate in California in 1994, sent out a campaign mailer with the inflammatory *Newsweek* cover of O.J. and Nicole captioned, "Living in Terror." It was crass, tasteless, and cynical. It was criticized by political analysts. It worked. Despite having three seemingly impossible strikes against her—liberal, Democrat, and gay—she won.

Police, prosecutors, and the courts also came under renewed fire for not arresting and prosecuting violators. Police departments promised to revise their procedures and training methods to better handle domestic violence. District attorneys promised to beef up their domestic violence units and diligently prosecute assailants. Judges promised that they would lengthen the sentences of convicted domestic batterers.

This was certainly welcome. It appeared that the nation was finally taking domestic violence seriously. But there was a problem. O.J. was the sole poster boy for domestic violence. The danger was that this would reinforce the time-worn stereotype that black men were exclusively America's violent sexual offenders.

• • • • • • •

*B*ut why? O.J didn't create the issue of domestic violence. It was a problem in American society long before the public heard him hysterically shout at Nicole and a companion on the 911 tapes the LAPD and the Los Angeles City Attorney's Office released to the press. Gender-based spousal abuse cuts across racial, cultural, and class lines in America. Thousands of Anglo, Latino, and Asian males have been accused of physically battering women.

The testimonials about spousal abuse poured in from all corners. Women of prominence and wealth such as book editor Hedda Nussbaum and heiress Ann Scripps Douglass bitterly complained to *Harpers Bazaar* about their years of marital suffering at the hands of abusive spouses. *Jewish Currents* warned that spousal abuse was a serious problem in the Jewish community, and that many women kept silent in order to maintain the appearance of "a nice Jewish husband" and a "happy Jewish home." In Los Angeles, droves of Korean men were required by courts to attend violence prevention workshops. Korean Counseling Centers reported that seventy percent of their referrals were for domestic abuse. Many Korean men cling to the parochial, old country view that women must be submissive and deferential to men.

Much of the media continues to ignore, deliberately omit, or skew the coverage to minimize the sexual sins of many white men. Fairness and Accuracy In Reporting (FAIR), a media watchdog group, showed how. In an eight-month study in 1993 and 1994 of domestic violence coverage in the *San Francisco Chronicle* and *Examiner*, FAIR found that the papers underreported or trivialized domestic violence as "unexpected, out of character or inexplicable" when the assailants were white males.

A coalition of women's groups presented FAIR's finding to the newspapers' mostly middle-class male editors and wealthy publishers. They acknowledged that the newspapers needed "a new formula" for reporting on violence against women. The publishers didn't indicate when or if they would devise a "new formula." Even O.J. saw that the press had failed to overhaul its reporting standards on domestic violence. He called the issue "hot" and "newsworthy" because a celebrity, namely himself, was the accused. While O.J. correctly railed at the press for making him the evil symbol of spousal abuse, he also correctly conceded that "the public needs to be awakened to the issue."

• • • • • •

$T$he issue of sexual abuse and domestic violence goes much deeper than the biased race and gender whims of editors and publishers. These men did not consciously make O.J., and black men in general, the symbols of sexual misconduct. They didn't have to. Racial and sexual stereotypes are reinforced by years of custom and tradition. They got a huge boost by one event and one man.

During the 1980's, Feminists demanded stronger laws

against sexual abuse. They were mostly ignored. That changed when Anita Hill charged Clarence Thomas with sexual harassment. Courts, legislatures, government, and corporate agencies scrambled to clarify sexual abuse and toughen laws.

This also raised a warning flag. Thomas complained that Hill's accusation played to the worst stereotype of black men as sex-crazed brutes. He was self-serving. He was desperate. He was playing on guilt. He was right. His words resonated in the ears of America. It touched off tremors in the psyches of many African-Americans who knew the tragic history of the sexual taboo and the physical and psychic damage that it wreaked on American society.

It didn't matter. Sexual harassment and Clarence Thomas became eternally linked in the public mind. After he finished taking the ceremonial oath of office and walked down the marble steps, a small band of protesters booed him and shouted, "Down with the male Supremacist Court."

Several months later he was scheduled to judge a moot court competition at Seton Hall University. He canceled when a women's student group threatened to hold a candlelight vigil. Thomas was a marked man, but for the wrong reason. His stone-age court opinions and votes on abortion, prisoners' rights, voting rights, school prayer, and affirmative action bordered on legal lunacy and judicial absurdity. He boasted that right-wing talk show hero, Rush Limbaugh, was his best running buddy and surrounded himself with an entourage of fanatical Christian fundamentalists.

However, when women's groups made Thomas and not

Oregon Senator Bob Packwood, the poster boy for sexual harassment, a color-free gender issue was hijacked. A close comparison of Thomas vs. Packwood shows why. One woman, Anita Hill, accused Thomas of sexual harassment. Twenty-nine women accused Packwood of the same. The women were employees, former employees, lobbyists, and campaign workers. Twenty-three of them swore to the *Washington Post* that Packwood tweaked, fondled, grabbed, and smooched them whenever and wherever.

If no one believed them, Packwood's kiss-and-tell diary might have confirmed it. He waged a hard legal battle to keep it from the public. He lost. But the question was, what would the Senate Ethics Committee do with it, and about him?

The Senate delayed, debated, and pondered. But ultimately, with a sex scandal brewing, women's groups watching and so many smoking guns, the Senate promised to pursue the investigation. The Committee emphasized that the probe would be for possible ethics violations and not sexual misconduct. If there was evidence of guilt, Packwood would not be expelled, only reprimanded.

There was no mass movement in the Senate to get rid of him. Only a half-dozen Democrats called for his resignation. (The rest were silent, perhaps worried that a full-scale investigation might rattle a few sexual skeletons in their own political closets.)

Senators weren't the only ones hibernating on Packwood. Within moments after Hill testified against Thomas, leaders of every national women's organization marched in angry lockstep to the Capitol. They demanded that the Senate Judiciary Committee reject Thomas's nomination. Their silence on Packwood was astonishing.

In May 1995, nearly two years later, the Senate Ethics Committee kept its promise and resuscitated the fossilized investigation. It concluded that there was "substantial credible evidence" of ethical and sexual misconduct by Packwood. It did not immediately recommend any punishment. The Committee promised to give him as many weeks as he needed to prepare his defense. There were still no widespread demands that he resign his chair of the Senate Finance Committee or Senate seat.

While O.J. had no political party to back him, nor political chits to call in, he had wealth and celebrity status. This gave him a small shield against adverse public scrutiny. But there was a strong hint that even this might not serve him like Packwood's political rank served him.

As the prosecution wound down its case against O.J., Anita Hill appeared in the courtroom. She was invited as a "guest" of the Los Angeles County District Attorney's Office. The DA gave no reason for her appearance and Hill did not offer any. It wasn't necessary. Hill is the universal symbol of the sexual harassment victim. Simpson is the universal symbol of the domestic violence abuser. Perhaps prosecutors hoped that her mere presence would be enough to damn O.J. in the eyes of the jurors and the public.

• • • • • •

*H*ill's appearance at the O.J. trial did not let Thomas off the hook. He had neither Packwood's political clout nor O.J.'s celebrity status. Two years after his confirmation he was still on the sexual hot seat. Hill was the issue. In *Strange Justice*, two female *Wall Street Journal* staff writers, Jane Myers and Jill Abramson, claimed that Thomas lied in his testimony to the Senate Judiciary Committee about his sexual conduct. They produced four women who claimed that Thomas was a sexual panderer. Thomas refused to respond. It was still their word against his. *Newsweek* thought enough of the book to excerpt a section from it, but conceded that the women's accusations were "impossible to verify."

Why did they drag this up more than two years after Thomas's confirmation? The writers claimed the point was to demonstrate that Thomas had betrayed the public trust and confidence and was not fit to serve on the bench. If so, why didn't Myers and Abramson focus on how the Judiciary Committee suppressed testimony that would expose Thomas's duplicity on affirmative action, voting rights, employment discrimination, capital punishment, and abortion rights? While the authors were ripping Thomas apart, did they also condemn Packwood? Not exactly. They approvingly acknowledged that the "maverick" Senator did not toe the Republican party line and vote to confirm Thomas.

Once again it came down to Hill. The authors, their publisher, the media, and the public fixated on the alleged sexual perversion of a prominent African-American. This was indeed strange justice.

The Thomas-O.J.-Packwood contrast stood out like a naked national sore. Thomas was politically incorrect for most civil rights activists and feminists. O.J. was a fallen idol and a tabloid obsession. Packwood was a politically correct, privileged, and publicly esteemed elected official.

Thomas represented a racial stereotype. O.J. represented celebrity, passion and prejudice. Packwood represented institutional power. For nearly two years, the Senate and the GOP closed ranks to protect and soften the punishment against one of its own. During that time, much of the media downplayed the Packwood story and the general public quickly lost interest. Packwood's accusers and their activist women supporters stirred barely a ripple with the public and lawmakers. There is no record that Hill showed up on Capitol Hill to protest sexual harassment when the Senate finally pondered Packwood's fate.

The spectre of Hill continued to haunt Thomas as he busily garnered mostly negative media reviews for his destructive opinions in controversial Supreme Court rulings on race, politics, and gender issues. The O.J. case became the flashpoint for national debate on domestic violence and racial issues.

• • • • • •

O.J. didn't mention him by name, but undoubtedly had more than a passing interest in the sad saga of defendant Mike Tyson. Both were superstar athletes and both were reviled by much of the public for, in Tyson's case, a sexual crime; in

Simpson's case, a domestic abuse crime linked to the murder charge. Tyson had also edged out William Kennedy Smith as the poster boy for date rape. Tyson seemed like a better choice than either Thomas or O.J. for a dubious sexual misconduct award. Thomas was a conservative Republican with no public history of sexual harassment before Hill's accusations. O.J. was an all-American sports hero with a squeaky clean public image. Tyson was sport's perennial "bad boy." But there was a problem.

It appeared that date rape was a frequent crime committed by young white males often on college campuses. Yet the Bureau of Justice declared that date rape occurred with "relative infrequency." Some even made excuses by insisting that the issue was mostly a propaganda ploy by women's groups to advance a narrow feminist agenda.

There were no debates, doubts, or apologetics about Iron Mike on the issue of date rape. Much of the press, the public, and those who ran the criminal justice system already made up their mind about him long before he put a foot in the courtroom. He was guilty. His trial and conviction in March 1992, for raping beauty queen contestant, Desiree Washington, was a formality. Iron Mike was "Bad Nigger" Jack Johnson reincarnated. His well-publicized scrapes with the law, marital troubles, sexual escapades, and thuggish behavior played to the old racial stereotypes.

Tyson didn't help his case. He told one interviewer, "If I wasn't in boxing, I'd be breaking the law." During the trial his defense attorneys depicted him as a thug, lecher, grabber, and womanizer, and reasoned since it was his public image, the jurors might not believe Washington was an innocent victim. She should have known what would happen if she went to his room.

This was a monumental blunder. Tyson did have an image as a brute. But the defense forgot that even brutes are held accountable for their actions. The jurors did not forget and the prosecution quickly seized the advantage. This modern-day Jack Johnson's goose wasn't cooked. It was scorched. As a convicted felon, Tyson was demonized. Sports writers in a legal postmortem reminded the public that Tyson was really a "boy within the brute." Another writer observed that the public shouldn't expect more from men who were "animalistic."

History had repeated itself. Another black heavyweight champion had committed a sexual crime. Desiree Washington, like Hill, was practically canonized as a selfless feminine martyr. Washington was no babe in the woods. There were serious questions about her version of the events and conduct on that fateful night.

Immediately after Tyson's release from prison in March 1995, at least five jurors who voted to convict him evidently had a change of mind about Washington. They told reporters that they believed that she was less than truthful in her testimony. It didn't matter. The issue of date rape and Mike Tyson are now indelibly linked in many people's minds. A bitter Tyson blamed society for turning him into a punching bag. "They pay $500 to see me. There's so much hypocrisy in the world."

In his prime, Tyson was society's primal force gladiator. He made big bucks for promoters and assorted hangers-on. He made good copy for sportswriters. He delighted a doting and fawning public. But, Mike took full advantage of that hypocrisy. He believed he *was* Iron Mike, a man above the law who could do anything and get away with it.

Mike was right about one thing. In the years before his arrest, society loved to see him perform, but it didn't love him. Society didn't guide him, educate him, and insist he become a productive and responsible role model. As for the few who did try, he probably didn't listen to them anyway. By the time he realized where he was headed, it was too late. Ultimately, the one most responsible for Mike Tyson's downfall was Mike Tyson.

But he was fortunate, he got a second chance. O.J. was confident that he would too.

• • • • • •

Michael Jackson was another mega-celebrity star who seemed to get a second chance. A smash interview with ABC-*Prime Time Live* in June 1995 and a new monster best selling album marked him as a man whose image had been publicly rehabilitated. But was it? Two years earlier, Jackson had been the poster boy for child sexual abuse. O.J. empathized with him. He blasted the media for creating a nightmare for Jackson based on the unsubstantiated word of a thirteen-year-old. This was not simply a case where one celebrity in trouble identified with another one in trouble. O.J. saw a little bit of himself in the way Jackson was treated.

Was Jackson a victim of tabloid lynching? A case could be made by contrasting his treatment to that of Paul Reubens AKA Pee Wee Herman. Herman did not molest a child. He molested himself at the Triple X-rated South Trail Cinema in Sarasota, Florida in 1991. But Herman made his name and fortune with his "Pee Wee's Playhouse" on CBS. He played father-clown surrogate to millions of children (and parents).

When the scandal broke, CBS fired him. Companies dumped him as a product spokesman. The media and the public didn't. There were no angry editorials (only amused quips). Children's advocate and parent groups were not outraged over his act, but over his treatment. Hundreds picketed the CBS offices in New York. They called the press coverage "unfair" and demanded that CBS rehire him. AKA Herman had tapped the public nerve. Millions probably thought the man had suffered enough.

A year later, Herman was on the comeback trail. He was making public appearances and formed a partnership to do public service ads for a drug-free America. The children's playhouse might not have been open again, but Herman was back in business.

It took longer with Michael. Almost immediately after the unnamed thirteen-year-old accused Jackson of sexual abuse in 1993, the media and much of the public turned vicious. Product sponsors and promotional appearance contracts vanished.

The man who had scrupulously avoided racial and political controversy and kept out of sight when not on stage performing, suddenly had touched off a national debate over child sexual abuse. Why Jackson?

Child abuse, even more than wife battering, sexual harassment, and rape is America's deepest and dirtiest secret. In 1992, there were nearly three million reported child abuse cases nationally, triple the number reported a decade ago. Most were "routine" cases of neglect, abandonment, or physical mistreatment. But 580,000 were sexual abuse reports. Although most of the cases were eventually tossed out because of insufficient evidence, and only ten percent of the allegations resulted in criminal prosecution, this only heightened the suspicion that more people than the public suspected were doing evil things to their children behind their household doors.

In a cover story a year after the Jackson controversy, *U.S. News & World Report* asked: "Sexual Predators: Can They Be Stopped?" The story focused on what communities were doing to combat child molesters. All the pictures were of white males. But where were their features and stories on them during the Jackson controversy? This might have countered the public perception that child sexual abuse wasn't an American problem, but a black problem. And this is far more important than whether O.J. felt that he and Jackson were being unfairly tried and convicted in and by the media.

• • • • • •

*O*.J. spotted and commented on another case in which he

believed the racial and sexual double-standards jumped out. In October 1994, Union, South Carolina housewife, Susan V. Smith, claimed that a black man jumped in her car, attacked her, and kidnapped her two children.

It was an American horror. A violent black man threatening innocent whites. A shocked and grieving public held prayer vigils, sent letters and telegrams, and dotted their homes with yellow ribbons. Hundreds of police and volunteers scoured the nearby woods searching for the missing boys. Police agencies nationwide were alerted.

President Clinton expressed sympathy for the family and the townspeople. Much of the media quickly latched onto the story. There were editorials and columns on the kidnapping. Police "Wanted" posters depicting a fearsome looking black male wearing a skull cap were plastered in newspapers and on TV screens during nightly newscasts.

The pattern was almost identical to the infamous Charles Stuart case in 1989 in Boston. Stuart murdered his pregnant wife, shot himself, and blamed it on a black man. Boston newspapers ran sensationalist stories on black crime. Politicians screamed for the death penalty, the police conducted draconian sweeps in black neighborhoods, and the public was terrified. Stuart was exposed and later committed suicide.

Smith confessed that she drowned her two children. The media did not intend to admit that it had again rushed to judgment on this one. Newspaper and TV reports quickly dropped the black-man-did-it angle. *Time* and *Newsweek*, in a self-congratulatory mood, claimed that the media, the public, and the police had learned from the Stuart case and did not overreact.

*Newsweek* missed the point. The issue was not whether the police indiscriminately shook down black men. (Thirty-five black men were questioned. Some were made to take lie detector tests.) Nor was the issue that the press ranted hysterically about black crime.

Smith failed two lie detector tests and refused to meet with a psychologist. She stuck by her story for nine days. Much of the public, the press, and the police believed her. But the same rules apply to child abuse (or murder) as domestic violence. When a wife or husband is murdered the spouse is always the prime suspect. In the majority of cases the spouse committed the murder.

Since 1976, 1,300 children have been killed annually by their parents or caretakers. Between 1988 and 1992, ninety-five children were killed in South Carolina by their parents or caretakers. More than half of them were killed by their mothers.

The questions were:

- Why wasn't Smith the prime suspect?
- Why would a black man kidnap Smith's children? Neither she, nor her family, were rich or famous. There was no ransom possibility.
- Where could a black man hide with two white children?
- Why did it take nearly a week for the media and law enforcement to begin to publicly question her story?

O.J. asked those same questions. He again blamed the

media for whipping up public anger "against this unknown black man." He was not completely right. As pointed out, not all the media bought Smith's yarn. The press did not play up the Smith tragedy to convict a black man as O.J. implied. It was news, and the public was fascinated by it. And that always spells dollars.

When Smith confessed, the media shifted gears and drove home a new angle. She was depicted as an emotionally disturbed woman, distraught over money problems, a failed marriage, and a disappointing romance. She was not called a "beast," "animal," or "savage" by the public or in the media. The issue for the media was no longer racism, but parents who murder their children.

Smith faced a two-count, first degree murder indictment and the prospect of a trial in South Carolina, an avid death penalty state. Yet the prosecutor agonized for weeks before finally deciding to seek the death penalty. Many South Carolinians were still willing to give her the benefit of the doubt. Said one, "We know her. We just can't see something like that happening to her." Smith, said another, would always be "the girl next door."

There was still a chance that Smith's ultimate punishment would not fit the crime. A 1994 Department of Justice study noted that parents "were the most likely to have had voluntary or non-negligent manslaughter as the most serious charge." Juries and judges were lenient with them because they refused to believe or admit that parents could kill their own children.

If the killer-kidnapper had been a black man, how would

the press have described him? Would the judge have been concerned about his fragile mental state or aberrant family history and have given his attorney maximum leeway on a plea? Would a jury have shown any sympathy if the answers were "no"? The answers should have been "no" for Smith.

The Smith trial could have publicly uncovered the dirty linen of domestic violence, mental abuse, child abandonment, and parental molestation in suburbia and small town America. The court made sure that it didn't. The judge banned TV cameras from the trial to "protect" the community. He had the perfect rationale—the O.J. trial. "The actors in the O.J. Simpson case were to a large extent just that—actors—Hollywood people who live in Hollywood because they wanted to be in the public eye." This was silly, flippant, and self-serving. But the judge correctly sensed the public mood on Smith. She was tried, convicted, and sentenced in a week. She got life in prison. The jurors at no point ever seriously considered the death penalty. Said one, she was just "a sick person."

The Smith case dropped from the media and public view the week after her sentencing. Smith represented an image that much of America would just as soon forget. Meanwhile, the Simpson case continued to be the subject of endless media and public discussion, debate and speculation. Simpson represented an image that much of America accepted and reveled in.

O.J. was right in lamenting the fact that media and public belief does not always reflect reality. Domestic violence, child sexual abuse, sexual harassment, and date rape are national problems. Trading in one-dimensional sexual stereotyping allows American society to absolve itself of collective blame. If sexual misconduct or crimes by white or non-black men are punished lightly or judged by a different standard, then women will continue to be at risk from male sexual violence and abuse. O.J.'s. face shouldn't be the only one on America's domestic violence poster.

## *three*
# The Tabloid Obsession

"What has hurt me the most is that in covering this story, the legitimate press became the 'tabloid press'." O.J. shouldn't have been too surprised by this. After all, this was the same press that made him one of America's favorite corporate pitchmen and superstar celebrities. From the start, he was ripe for the tabloid pickings of that press.

These were early examples. "Friends say he pursued other women freely." "He ordered Nicole back to her parents so he could play the field." "He was seen at decorous orgies snorting cocaine." The quotes about O.J. were not from the *National Enquirer*, *Star*, or the *Examiner*. They were from *Time* and *Newsweek*. They depicted him as a dangerous, sexually-out-of-control drug user.

For decades these two staid publications have set the standards for journalistic integrity. They crossed into tabloid land with O.J. It was an easy journey to make. The TV networks had made it with *Hard Copy*, *Inside Edition*, and the mountain of daytime sleazy talk shows. They had swapped professionalism for kinky tantalization.

*Time* and *Newsweek* borrowed the techniques perfected by the baser tabloid journalists. The revelations about Simpson were made by unnamed "sources," "friends," "acquaintances," "associates," and "colleagues." There was no independent substantiation or official confirmation of any of their allegations. Tabloids use this method to titillate. Mainstream publications use it to frame or shape public opinion.

Editors and publishers routinely sneak their personal or political opinions into a story by attributing damning information to "unnamed sources." Their excuse is that the information is so critical and revealing that they must protect the confidentiality of their informants. Their informants pretend to be public spirited individuals motivated solely by conscience and the desire to tell the truth. More often the "sources" are selected, if not invented, to validate a point of view or story line the editors already dictated.

Often the "sources" are self-serving individuals who harbor personal jealousies, grudges, or hatreds. Some are driven simply by plain old-fashioned greed. They gladly tell reporters what they want to hear. The *Washington Post, New York Times, L.A. Times, Wall Street Journal, Chicago Tribune, USA Today,* and other major newspapers use anonymous or "unnamed" sources to allow political leaders to put their spin on events.

The major newsweeklies took the tabloid's favorite obsessions: sex, drugs, violence, the antics of high profile celebrities, and eagerly applied their smut techniques to O.J. Soon the mainstream media and the tabloids became indistinguishable.

Let's compare.

A headline in the *Star* screamed, "O.J.'s Sex and Drug Parties." The "revelation" did not come from an "unnamed source" but rather a disgruntled former LAPD officer. He claimed that he participated in wild sex orgies and marathon coke snorting sessions at Simpson's home. The *Star* demanded that readers suspend disbelief and imagine that an ordinary beat cop would be invited to share in the debauchery of a nationally known celebrity.

At least the *Star* had the decency to name the snoop. *Newsweek* didn't. "The Double Life of O.J. Simpson," in the August 1994, *Newsweek* "found" that O.J. "cruised bars" and "indulged in drugs and random sex." It did not name any source. In two other references to Simpson's alleged drug and sex romps, the informants were "sources" or "friends." There was no independent confirmation from a named source.

• • • • • •

The *National Enquirer* dug out its "sources" and discovered a witness to the killing: "I saw O.J. at the murder scene." According to the "source," Los Angeles County District Attorney Gil Garcetti was keeping the witness under deep wraps. There was no independent confirmation from the District Attorney's Office that such a witness existed. While *Time* lacked the headline flair of the *Enquirer*, it didn't skimp on gossip: "Some discern a classic love triangle." Based on the testimony of "some," *Time* implied that the love triangle spelled motive and murder.

The *Examiner* jumped into the act with a "world exclusive" interview purportedly with Nicole's father. He claimed that O.J. refused to tell his children that he was in jail. This shouldn't surprise anyone. The man *Time* and *Newsweek* branded a womanizer and drug user could hardly be expected to be a responsible parent. It played to the old stereotype of the irresponsible black male.

*Newsweek* didn't stop with O.J. It dredged up an alleged "friend" who claimed that Nicole wasn't much good at parenting either. In a companion feature, she was shown standing in a late model open top sports car surrounded by her kids. The caption read: "Fast Laner: Making Time for Sydney and Justin." We're also told that "she feared that he was too critical of their daughter." *Newsweek* didn't explain whether this might simply be a normal parental concern. The word "feared" was left to dangle ominously in the public mind.

It didn't dangle long. *Newsweek* made an accusation that even the tabloids didn't. When Simpson was arrested, the reporters pestered his first wife, Marguerite, for an interview. They probably prayed that she'd reveal that he abused her, too. She didn't. So *Newsweek* dredged up an interview purportedly done with her in 1968. In the interview, she allegedly called him a "beast."

There was no indication who did the interview or where it was published. "Beast" was a loaded code word. It was not put in context. Did she mean his personality? His conduct? His attitude? Or his treatment toward her? Readers could draw their own conclusions.

Neither Marquerite nor anyone else who had intimate knowledge of their relationship claimed that O.J. physically abused her. He paid child support and agreed to a generous property settlement. Marquerite made no public charges of abuse or misconduct about or against him at any time during or after their marriage. The only interview of public record that she ever gave during her marriage to O.J. was in 1968 after he won the Heisman Trophy. She told the *Daily Trojan*, "Mostly everyone sees him as the big football star, smiling and signing autographs, to me he is a husband."

The prosecution, like *Newsweek*, ignored this. They publicly announced that they would subpoena her to testify at the trial that O.J. physically abused her during their marriage. But Marquerite was one step ahead of them. At the start of the trial, she told ABC-TV's *20/20* news program, "No, he did not (abuse me). There was no way that I would allow that to happen to me." Prosecutors got the message. They did not summon her. Still *Newsweek* used her and its legion of "unnamed sources" to type O.J. as a cocaine driven, sexual madman.

• • • • • •

*I*f *Time* and *Newsweek* were no different than the tabloids in the O.J. case, there's a reason. The *National Enquirer*, *Star*, the *Examiner*, and the other tabloids have successfully parlayed gossip, innuendo, rumor, half-truths, and outright lies into hugely profitable empires. They have millions of devoted readers. Their market continues to expand. More people read the tabloids than read the *L.A. Times, New York Times,* or *Washington Post.* More Americans get their "news" from *Hard Copy* and *Rescue 911* rather than from the three major network evening news programs.

TV network executives and major newspaper editors deny that they have turned much of the public into gossip junkies. They claim they give the public the type of information and programming that it wants.

In 1995, much of America's media business was tightly controlled by fewer than twenty corporations. When Westinghouse gobbled up CBS, it got fifteen TV stations that reached thirty-two percent of the nation's households, and thirty-nine radio stations with an almost forty percent share of the listener market. Congress almost certainly will pass legislation that will let more corporations own even more media outlets. If the present trend continues, and there's no reason to think it won't, the media will soon be a wholly owned subsidiary of wealthy corporate investors.

Even now they directly influence the decisions of senior editors and producers on program selection and news slants. If they decided that the public had an insatiable appetite for tidbits of rumor and gossip about O.J. and Nicole's private lives, that's what the public got.

The real issue is, as always, how high can the ratings be shoved and how much profit can be milked out of journalistic muck. As it turns out, a lot. In 1994, O.J. was featured in fifty-four cover stories in the weekly magazines. The *National*

*Enquirer* splattered O.J. gossip on twenty-one of twenty-seven cover stories and weekly sales soared to an estimated 500,000.

*Newsweek, Time, People, U.S. News & World Report, Sports Illustrated, Atlantic Monthly,* and the *New Yorker* made up the rest of the elite magazine pack that heard the cash registers jingling and splashed O.J. across their covers. This in itself is not evil or malicious. News gathering is a business and sensational news does sell. Magazine advertisers depend on those increased sales to more effectively market their products. Publishers run the stories and features that they think will enhance sales to attract greater ad revenue.

But that also presents a problem. In the past, magazines and newspapers that covered celebrated, even sensational, court cases played it close-to-the-vest with their accounts. Reporters stuck to the facts and the testimony. They resisted the temptation to editorialize, swap gossip, or reduce the case to a contest of personalities. They reported on the testimony, deliberations, and the final verdict. When the trial ended, they interviewed the prosecutor, the defense attorney(s), and perhaps a juror or two. They refrained from second-guessing or offering ill-formed opinions about the verdict or the case. The public generally got a good factual story, *sans* sensationalism.

No more. The tabloids left their gossipy marks everywhere in the O.J. case. Deputy District Attorney Christopher A. Darden, for instance, was not embarrassed to reveal that he had acted on a tip from a *Star* reporter that one of the jurors had once met O.J. at a Hertz-sponsored open house. The juror was dismissed. The defense was surprised that the *Star* suddenly had that kind of credibility. Superior Court Judge Lance A. Ito, however, didn't think it was especially bizarre. He was almost right.

The tabloids exploited the O.J. case for cash. They did not pretend that they were informing or educating the public. Mainstream publishers did. They kidded themselves that they were noble benefactors satisfying the public's need to know about O.J.

When the *New York Times* got caught with its journalistic covers down after using the *Enquirer* as a source for a story, it self-righteously wailed that journalists had the right to get their facts from whatever source, tainted or not. *Newsweek* tried to have its cake and eat it, too. It smugly blasted the media for running endless stories short on fact and long on sleaze that stoked the public's lurid fascination with the case. It then promptly turned around and blamed that same public for turning into dim-wits on world events. *Newsweek* did not say whether it considered its own cover stories—"The Double Life of...," "The Case against...," "The Trial..."(complete with a ghost-like silhouette of Nicole superimposed behind O.J.), and others riddled with speculation and gossip from "unnamed sources"—as models of journalistic integrity.

If the legitimate media occasionally turned tabloid to destroy what remained of the reputation and image of a celebrity, and further jade the public about the media and the criminal justice system to get that extra profit, it was deemed a small price to pay.

Some hope that an increasingly cynical and fearful public

will say enough is enough and turn off. This is doubtful. Much of the media will continue to produce, package, and sell gossip, titillation, and stereotypes as news. They are durable, convenient, and highly profitable. As long as the majority of Americans depend exclusively on the major media for their news, they will continue to believe them.

From his jail cell, a bitter and disillusioned O.J. lashed out at the tabloid press, "As long as O.J. is the suspect, this story is money. They wouldn't be doing this story if it wasn't for money." O.J., in his heyday, feasted off that press, and became wealthy. If O.J. was being somewhat disingenuous, he could be excused. Even he deserved better.

## four
# The Real Menace to Society

O.J. Simpson had not been formally charged with any crime. He had just returned to his Rockingham Avenue estate from a business trip to Chicago. Less than twenty-four hours earlier he had been informed that his ex-wife, Nicole Brown Simpson, and Ronald Goldman had been murdered. Yet in full view of a small army of reporters and banks of TV cameras, the superstar stood surrounded by LAPD officers with his hands cuffed behind his back. Donald Thompson, the LAPD officer who slapped the cuffs on him, said that he was ordered by a detective to "cuff him." He claimed that the handcuffing was appropriate and that he was following procedure. He wasn't. LAPD Chief Willie Williams later made it clear that it was not department policy to cuff someone who was not under arrest.

For that instant the LAPD rushed to judgment and presumed him guilty of a crime. He was momentarily treated like a "gangsta." The handcuffs were a painful reminder that Simpson's wealth and fame did not entirely shield him from the stereotype that black men suspected of a crime are automatically guilty. He had come full circle back to his troubled past. Three decades earlier the teenaged Simpson ran with a street gang. He stole hubcaps, pillaged liquor stores, and got into gang brawls. Eventually he wound up in a youth detention center.

Simpson was unrepentant. When police demanded his identification, he told them his name was "Burt Lancaster." Simpson later bragged, "I was really putting one over, a teenage black kid fooling the establishment." Only a brash and foolish young smart aleck could really believe that. The police are not in the business of being fooled by African-Americans. Neither is American society. The handcuffed Simpson was a stark reminder of that.

He's not alone. Black businessmen and professionals complain that security guards follow them and clerks closely watch them, in grocery and department stores. They complain that they are stopped by the police when driving late model cars, questioned, frisked, and that their cars are searched. They complain that women clutch their purses and reverse direction when they approach. They complain that motorists slam down the locks on their car doors when they stop beside them at traffic signals.

Midway through the O.J. trial, Willie Cravin found out that the courtroom where he had deliberated as a juror for six months was no sanctuary from stereotypes. Prosecutors, his non-black jury peers, and Judge Lance Ito claimed that the soft-spoken, devout, Bible-reading postal services supervisor, "intimidated" a non-black female juror. Ito charged Cravin with seven acts of "intimidating" other jurors. The non-black juror said that Cravin "stared" at her in an elevator. She said she felt frightened and uncomfortable. Cravin was unceremoniously bounced from the jury.

A dumbfounded Cravin screamed foul and charged that he was ousted not because of anything he did but because of some "fool-headed stereotype." There was no guesswork as to what he meant. He was a big, no-nonsense man who much of society deemed fit the prototype of a menacing black. And that apparently included Ito who made special note of his large size. "I felt like the jury was on trial," said Cravin, "not the Juice." He was wrong. The jury wasn't on trial. Cravin was. He violated the unwritten rule of racial etiquette by not presenting the eternally pleasing, happy-go-lucky demeanor seemingly required of black men.

• • • • • •

While Cravin was not a criminal, crime, nonetheless, is an intensely personal and emotional issue for those victimized. The trauma is deep and the memories cause perpetual pain for the victims and their families. It stirs the deepest human fears and vulnerabilities. When racial and sexual stereotypes are mixed in, personal fear becomes public hysteria.

A study on reader perception of crime reported in the *Chicago Tribune* found that in several crime-related stories the paper mentioned that the suspect was a white male under age twenty-five. Many readers still identified the suspect as a black male under age twenty-five.

This is more than a case of warped perceptions of crime. The political ad run during the 1988 presidential election by George Bush on escaped black convict Willie Horton was jammed with hidden racial messages. But the ad did more than pander to racist fears and help put Bush in the White House. When a control group of whites was shown the campaign footage that included part of the Horton ad, they were asked if they felt more threatened by crime or perceived another message? The other message was race. The ad hardened the participants not only toward criminals but to all blacks. They were less inclined to spend more money on social programs to aid blacks and the poor.

There is one exception. Americans are willing to spend more to lock them up. America's prison population has nearly doubled from 900,000 in 1987 to 1.4 million in 1994. The prison-industrial complex has replaced the nearly defunct military-industrial complex as America's largest growth industry.

The O.J. case gave a horrid glimpse of the ballooning cost of crime and punishment in America. The state spent an estimated $10 million to jail and try him. O.J. faced the almost certain prospect of spending the rest of his life in a new cell. In California there will be plenty. State taxpayers will pay twenty-one billion dollars over the next thirty years to build twenty-five new prisons. While they will pay $1.8 billion to run their eight campuses of the University of California system, they will spend $5 billion to run their prisons. Construction companies, contractors, architectural firms, and lobbyists will make billions. Wall Street will rake in a neat thirty-five million dollars from the sale of California's $5.6 billion in lease revenue bonds the legislature floated without taxpayer approval.

What will this buy? The Rand Corporation claims the money will reduce felonies by only eight percent. The vast majority who will fill the new jail cells won't be violent felons though. They will be poor blacks and Latinos who commit mostly property or drug-related crimes. Most will not have the use of a stationary bike, be permitted two hours of daily private TV viewing, have the exclusive access to a phone, and be regularly fed hot meals. These were the privileges that celebrity O.J. had during much of the time that he spent in L.A. County jail.

Rand doesn't state that if California taxpayers spent a fraction of the three strikes budget on drug counseling, vocational job and skills training, education, and violence reduction programs that many black, Latino and poor defendants might not be in those cells.

• • • • • •

Crime is also not race neutral. The gangster attraction and image of the young, poor Simpson, or the handcuffing of the rich and famous Simpson were powerful images that reflect the dangerous cycle of arrest and incarceration of black males. The cycle traps thousands. One out of four young black men are in jail or prison, on parole or probation. Nearly half of America's one million prisoners are black. The top-heavy number of black men in jail reinforces the public view that they commit most of the major violent crime in America.

They don't. In 1992:

- White males committed fifty-four percent of violent crimes in America.
- White males were seventy percent of the juveniles arrested nationally for criminal offenses.
- White males were eighty percent of America's drug users and abusers.
- White males committed sixty percent of the urban hate crimes.
- White males committed the majority of serial and mass murders.

This last point deserves special comment. I wonder why much of the media, the public and sociologists aren't as obsessed with the serial murders committed mostly by white males as they are with black crime. I did a computer scan of four hundred academic journals between the years 1992 and 1994. There were 1,691 research articles published on crime.

Forty identifiable research articles dealt specifically with black crime. Two identifiable research articles dealt with serial/mass murders. The one detailed article on serial murders was published in a small journal, *The Omega-Journal of Death and Dying*. The authors admitted that there was a "poverty of rigorous research in the area."

The same can't be said about O.J. In a two and one-half month stretch before his trial, O.J. was mentioned 15,310 times in articles. There were 1,015 features and news reports on the

O.J. case from the time of his arrest through the first six months of his trial.

I also closely monitored the press reports on the prison murder of mass murderer Jeffrey Dahmer in November 1994. The media spin was sympathy and compassion for Dahmer. His mother tearfully made the talk show rounds. In the *L.A. Times* account, Dahmer's prosecutor, psychologist, defense attorney, and relatives were quoted. They recast him as a tragic figure.

The prosecutor thundered that "this is not justice." The psychiatrist called him "pleasant, polite, free of prejudice, and gentle." There was a brief quote from an attorney representing the family of one of his victims. There was only passing reference that fourteen out of his seventeen known victims were black men. The other three were Latino or Asian. Ironically, Dahmer had no sympathy for himself. His mother told an interviewer that "he felt that he deserves anything he gets."

• • • • • •

Suburban whites may have nightmares about being attacked by blacks, but their waking reality is that their attacker will be white. In 1990, seventy percent of violent crimes against whites were committed by other whites. But just who gets punished and who doesn't often gets tangled in a web of prejudice and negative stereotypes. LAPD detective Mark Fuhrman, courtesy of the Simpson trial, became America's poster boy for the racist cop. He did nothing to help the cause of those who insist that law enforcement is unbiased when he decided to be the prime role player in a series of audiotape interviews on police practices.

The would-be "actor" told a documentary filmmaker that some LAPD officers take great delight in giving black motorists the "attitude test." To pass, blacks must be properly deferential and respectful; presumably this means they cannot question or challenge an officer who stops them no matter what the reason. If they fail the test, said Fuhrman, officers might destroy their license and arrest them. Fuhrman stepped even further beyond the bounds of police work when he openly boasted that he threatened to kill a suspect in the shooting of a police officer if he didn't "cooperate." It was legal thuggery of the highest order, but was any of it true? The Simpson defense team quickly latched onto this as "proof" that Fuhrman could have planted a bloody glove at O.J.'s Rockingham estate and that the LAPD conspired to "frame" O.J. Fuhrman's audio admissions may have been nothing but pure bunkum coming from an officer whose credibility was suspect and who was out to grab the limelight.

But it is no exaggeration to say that many black offenders do wind up behind bars, while many white offenders don't. Their increasing absence from the prisons is noticeable. A District of Columbia judge was curious to see what the jails were like that he sent defendants to. After he visited several, he was struck by the fact that most of those inside were black. He knew from his experience on the bench that many whites were charged with crimes. He wondered what happened to them.

There was a clue. Seventy-eight percent of the 580 white middle-class males convicted of defrauding savings and loans (and taxpayers) of nearly $8 billion went to prison during the early 1990's. Most didn't stay very long. Only four percent were sentenced to ten years or more. The average sentence was 36.4 months. The median time served was two years. A car thief spends 38 months in prison; a burglar, 55.6 months. In California, only one in four savings and loan fraud suspects was prosecuted. In Texas, one in seven was prosecuted. For those with money, personal and family connections, and political clout to avoid prison, crime did indeed pay.

The public veil often drawn over white crime sharply contrasted with the public and media obsession with O.J. This can bring deep pain to society. An attorney in Perry County, Oklahoma tragically observed: "It was just a matter of circumstance and luck that he hadn't been released yet." She was talking about Timothy McVeigh. The man accused of the bloodiest mass murder attack in American history, the April 1995 bombing of the federal building in Oklahoma City, came within an eyelash of walking out of the Perry County jail a free man. McVeigh was arrested for carrying an illegal, concealed weapon and driving without a license tag. This should have raised suspicion that he might be potentially dangerous.

Most police officers know that routine traffic stops often result in violent criminals being nabbed. In California, O.J.'s home state, more than half of the police pursuits begin with "routine" stops for traffic violations and wind up in felony arrests. That didn't happen with McVeigh. His bail was a ridiculously low $500. The county assistant district attorney saw nothing unusual about him. If not for a timely fax from federal authorities, McVeigh would have made bail.

He was young, a military hero and significantly, a white male, everything O.J. wasn't. In recent years, men like McVeigh who belong to or claim to have ties with militant militias and patriot groups have committed dozens of bank robberies, shot it out with the FBI, BATF officers, attacked federal land agents, stockpiled mounds of weapons, openly tested bombs, conducted military maneuvers and organized dozens of paramilitary groups in thirty states.

Their terrorist threats, tactics, criminal activities, and violence aren't the stuff of nightly *Action News* reports, press features, editorials, and exposes. They aren't singled out as a menace to society in national debates over crime, three strike laws, the death penalty, and more prison construction.

Dozens of local, state, and national officials liken these groups of mostly white men who call themselves militias and patriots to modern-day Paul Reveres fighting against government tyranny. Even in the aftermath of the Oklahoma City bombing there were no mass raids on their headquarters or roundups of their leaders. Clinton, Republican leaders, media commentators, and political analysts demanded that their civil rights and civil liberties be scrupulously observed.

Men like McVeigh got an automatic legal cushion. O.J. had to buy his.

• • • • • •

*S*impson's lead trial attorney, Johnnie L. Cochran, Jr., was concerned that America's fear of violent crime might wear O.J.'s legal cushion thin. "In truth and reality, our communities are fast becoming prisons without walls." Cochran spoke as a civil libertarian and an attorney battling to free America's most celebrated murder defendant.

Cochran also pointed to a major dilemma in America. While the fear, even paranoia, about violent crime is legitimate, and even understandable, few Americans really know how violent urban streets are. But *Newsweek*, in 1994, still punched the murder panic button hard. It warned that murder was epidemic and displayed gruesome photos of mostly young black and Hispanic male victims. But a cursory glance at *Newsweek's* numbers showed that Americans were actually at less risk of becoming murder victims in 1990 (9.5 per 100,000) than in 1980 (10.2 per 100,000). In fact, Americans actually stood a better chance of being murdered during the Prohibition-era in the 1920's than in 1994.

But crime is not an equal opportunity predator anyway. The richer, older, and whiter a person, the less chance he has of becoming a crime victim. Older white women are the least victimized of any group in America. Those who earn more than $50,000 are two to three times less likely to be crime victims than the general population. For whites aged fifty to sixty-four, the victim rate drops thirty-five percent compared to non-whites. Whites are marginally at greater risk of being robbed by blacks.

It has less to do with their color than their numbers and

location. There are seven times more whites than blacks in America. Most of them aren't robbed in their homes or neighborhoods but rather on urban streets.

The arrest totals for blacks are further inflated by police saturation of inner city neighborhoods, gang sweeps, drug raids, and racially-tainted "zero tolerance" stop and search policies. Compton, a Southern California city with a black and Latino majority and a nationwide "gangsta" reputation, went one better. In 1993, it criminalized every youth in the city. The police department's database contained the names of 10,435 gang members in the city. It was a curious figure.

The 1990 Census counted only 8,558 males aged fifteen to twenty-five in the city. There were three possible explanations: the database was faulty, the information was inputted incorrectly, or as one observer quipped, maybe Crip gang members moonlighted as Bloods gang members and vice versa.

Much of the public doesn't question these distortions. There are too many men like the young street tough O.J. to make them seem more than plausible. The press reached back thirty years, dug out O.J.'s juvenile record and later rash boasts about his gang past, and used them to reinforce the public image of him as an unreconstructed gang-banger. If the tag applied to him, many might think it could easily apply to all young blacks.

The O.J. case also helped feed the myth that the drug problem is largely a black problem. The unsupported press allegations that O.J. was a wild-living, cocaine-abuser went largely unchallenged. That was easy for many to believe since the only ones the public routinely saw being jailed for crack cocaine abuse and sale were young black males. Former Reagan administration drug czar William Bennett told why: "It's easier and less expensive to arrest black drug users and dealers than whites." The price is higher than he thinks. Bennett, much of the press, and lawmakers operate under the assumption that crack cocaine trafficking and abuse are solely black crimes. Congress responded to that public perception by making the minimum sentence longer for crack during the mid-1980's.

It's true that blacks are disproportionately more involved in crack dealing and are arrested more often. But many whites are also deeply involved in the crack trade and those arrested do have more serious criminal histories than blacks. Yet black crack traffickers still receive on average longer sentences than white crack traffickers.

A rash of government studies, newspaper reports, and features confirm there is indeed a savage dual standard in the federal prosecution of black crack users and dealers as opposed to white powdered cocaine users and dealers. Many judges, black community leaders and even some prosecutors and elected officials called for sentencing reform. Attorney General Janet Reno and Congress said "no." Clinton was silent on the issue but had plenty to say about the O.J. trial. He called it a "circus atmosphere." If it's a question of justice and fairness versus political expediency and public posturing, it's not hard to guess which will win out.

Even if blacks did commit most of the violent crime in America, most whites still wouldn't be at risk. According to official figures, blacks commit nearly half the murders and robberies. Ninety-four percent of their victims are other blacks. Blacks are mostly a menace not to society, but to themselves. When street tough O.J. bragged about being bad and beating up "the dudes that deserved it," he confirmed that.

• • • • • •

Simpson wasn't handcuffed merely because of biased law enforcement reports or a racially-tainted criminal justice system. His celebrity status provided him a slight edge in treatment over the average African-American. It did not provide him a clean escape from society's often criminal typecasting of black men. TV news and some shows have seen to that.

Ninety-five million TV viewers watched dozens of LAPD vehicles follow O.J. down the San Diego freeway in June 1994. There was a bloody double murder, domestic violence, and alleged sexual hijinks. It was the crowning moment for TV crime-verite. It was no accident. The TV networks had spent the past twenty years honing tabloid-style reporting techniques. During the 1970's, the men that ran the ABC affiliates in Philadelphia and New York decided to rev up the ratings. They created *Action News*.

The concept was simple: find crime, crime, and more crime. News teams roamed city streets looking for police car chases, crashes, gang shoot-outs, and drug busts. Most importantly, the city streets were in black neighborhoods. It was bloody. It was exploitative. It was racist. It was a smash success. The public loved it. Network profits jumped and their ratings soared. *Action News,* which began as a lead-in to the regular newscast, soon became *the* news. Local affiliates in every city copied it.

By 1990, sixty-eight percent of Americans were hooked on *Action News'* nightly broadcasts. The networks spun off legions of hybrid clones. These shows simulated live-action crime chases and busts. *Top Cops, Cops,* and *America's Most Wanted* often depicted whites as heroes and blacks as villains. This has convinced even more Americans that their lives are at grave risk from violence-prone, drugged out African-Americans.

They aren't. But many Americans still exaggerate black crime even when the crimes are committed by others. In 1992, in Los Angeles, O.J.'s home city, some TV reporters stretched credulity to the limits during the civil disturbances. For three days the black and increasingly brown inner city residents were judged by suburban, middle-class reporters, men and women. They lived far from the area, and in some cases needed maps to find the streets. These reporters relentlessly tailored their reports to depict the violence as the handiwork of black rioters. Racism, poverty, alienation, and the indifference of the city's political power structure were barely mentioned.

The reporters couldn't ignore the abominable verdict in the state trial of the four LAPD officers that beat Rodney King. But they made no serious effort to analyze the criminal justice system, explain why the jury contained no blacks, or discuss the racism that motivated the jury's decision. There was one passing reference in the *L. A. Times* to the negative remarks of the white jurors about King's physical prowess and alleged aggressive actions.

One juror even made a borderline racially derogatory remark about him and hinted that he got what he deserved. Hardly anyone second-guessed the inept and ineffectual prosecution strategy that practically tossed the case to the defense.

Instead some of the reporters stuck microphones and cameras in the face and mouth of any black they could find on the streets and deliberately framed questions to get sensational soundbites. They badgered their respondents to say something inflammatory. The networks repeatedly played the videotape of the young blacks beating white truck driver Reginald Denny, further inflaming fear and anger in the suburbs. The media's message to sympathetic whites was that the Denny beating canceled out the moral outrage over the King beating.

O.J., for one, insisted that he was not ready to forgive or forget what happened to King. The King beating apparently prompted a flashback to his young days and his own near violent confrontations with the police. There was little doubt that young tough O.J., who boasted of growing up in the streets and flirting with crime and gangs, would be at risk from police scrutiny. It would, however, take a strong imagination to believe that celebrity O.J. completely identified with a poor, ex-convict like King. Then again there was really no need to speculate about that. Celebrity O.J. admitted that he paid no attention to news stories of brutality or abuse involving blacks.

While O.J., pre-arrest, may have missed the underlying

racial angles in the King case and the civil disturbances, reporters, news anchors, and in-studio talking heads busily distorted them. But TV was an open mirror. Viewers could plainly see many of those doing the looting and burning were non-blacks. The streets at times looked like a microcosm of the United Nations.

A Rand Corporation study of the racial breakdown of 5,000 riot-related cases processed through Los Angeles municipal courts tallied these arrest totals: Latinos, 2,852; blacks, 2,037; Anglos, 601; and others, 147. Young men aged eighteen to thirty-four made up the highest percentage of those arrested (thirty percent). The number of whites arrested was nearly one-third of the total number of blacks arrested. The rioters were young men of all nationalities.

A Rand criminologist was puzzled by the fixation of the press on black rioters when the majority of those rioting weren't. "This was clearly not a black riot. It was a minority riot." The report appeared as a news item in the back pages of the *L. A. Times.* The rest of the press ignored it.

Simpson was not Rodney King. Yet several LAPD officers presumed King guilty of crimes he had not committed and physically beat him. Two were subsequently convicted in federal court. Simpson was presumed guilty of crimes he had not been charged with and handcuffed. The LAPD officer that put the cuffs on him was mildly reprimanded. But for that fleeting moment King and Simpson had one thing in common. They were two black men that much of America perceived as "gangstas."

• • • • • •

**W**orse, some black men act out that image.

Nicole: "My ex-husband has just broken into my house and he's ranting and raving outside in the front yard."
Dispatcher: "Has he been drinking or anything?"
Nicole: "No. But he's crazy."

In that moment of rage, O.J. turned the clock back thirty years. He was no longer the courtly, congenial celebrity. He was the young tough who ran with the Persian Warriors street gang in San Francisco. The target of celebrity Simpson's aggression was Nicole. The target of street tough O.J.'s aggression was other blacks. Celebrity O.J. was incredulous that his violent attack on her in 1989 drew the police. "And now you're going to arrest me for this?" Street tough O.J. bragged that his violence was accepted. "Nobody messed with me. O.J. was <u>ba-ad</u>."

Some men are consumed by the same rage as O.J. Many white males exhibit their aggression against each other in brawls at rock concerts, football games, fraternity houses, and bars. The root of male aggression is male privilege, class inequality, and personal alienation. The root of black male violence is the same. The special ingredient is racism.

During two centuries of slavery and a century of legal segregation, America's unwritten rule was that blacks could not strike back or vent anger against whites. This could bring a severe beating, prison term, or even death. Black-on-black violence was usually ignored or lightly punished by the authorities. This left deep psychic scars on many black men. The internalized anger was transformed into displaced aggression. Their targets were nearly always other blacks and often women. The consequences have been deadly.

Between 1980 and 1985, a staggering 44,428 black males were murdered. This nearly equals the number of American soldiers killed during the entire Vietnam conflict. Their assailants were not the police or white vigilantes but other black males. With the spread of the drug trade in African-American communities during the 1980's and 1990's, the murder rate inched upward. American society, it often appeared, expected, accepted, and didn't really give a damn about black violence as long as it didn't spill over the borders of the ghettos into suburbia.

Black leaders agonized over and launched internal soul searches to exorcise the demon of black violence. Their concern was genuine. Their hyperbole to describe it wasn't. Black violence is a compelling and deadly issue. But it can't be compared to the half-century of lynchings and mob violence. Black violence is internal, individual and causes personal pain. Racist violence was collective, systematic and designed to control and dehumanize blacks. The psychic scars and wounds are still present.

Much of black violence stems from the desperate search by some young black males for the identity and esteem that America systematically denies them. In an orderly society there is an unstated "mutual contract" between citizens. They must believe that the political institutions are just, and that the laws will protect them. They must believe that society will allow them opportunities to achieve and prosper. When they perceive that society has implicitly violated its social contract, they are suspended in a social void.

Some young blacks exist in a state of *anomie*, a French word that literally means normlessness. O.J., judging by his later boasts, brags, and taunts about his street life as a youth, seemed to fit into that category. In the context of American racism, this means that he, and others like him, have a sense of being removed from society's rules. Sociologists that measure *anomie* find that many young black males have a far stronger sense of social estrangement than white males. They create their own standards and behavior patterns that are separate and distinct from the socially approved goals of American society. This could include use of language, clothing styles and systematic defiance of authority.

Their tough talk, swagger, and mannerisms are the culturally adapted defense mechanisms many black males use to boost esteem. Some black males measure their status or boost esteem by demonstrating their proficiency in physical fights or the sexual abuse of black women.

The aggressive body language of some young black men has become their walking advertisement that states "don't mess with me if you want to stay healthy." From blues to rap music, the cowering, pitiful emasculated black man was transformed into the "bad nigger." His feats soared to mythic dimensions in the folklore, language, tradition and music of blacks. The legendary toughs of black folklore, Billy G. and Stackolee, were so bad they scared themselves.

"I've got a tombstone disposition and a graveyard mind. I know I'm a bad motherfucker that's why I don't mind dying."

For decades the exploits of bad black men were the stuff of song and tall tales told in work camps, pool rooms, bars, and later on in urban city streets. They sent men scurrying when they walked into bars. Anyone foolish enough to confront them got a busted jaw or a bullet in the chest. Whites created folk hero outlaws and desperadoes, and sung their praises. These men rebelled against corrupt society, had some socially redeeming value and always died heroic deaths. By contrast, there was an almost nihilistic quality to the violence perpetrated by bad black men on their black victims.

"Shoot nigger, shoot to kill. I'm so bad, I don't ever want to be good."

• • • • • •

$A$n accidental bump, an ill-spoken word, a prolonged stare from a stranger is often taken by insecure black males as an ego challenge or an affront to their "manhood." It could escalate into violence. In Ralph Ellison's *Invisible Man*, two black men were seated next to each other in a tavern. Violence nearly ensued when one asked another a simple question.

"Oh, take it easy," I growled. "A man can ask a question, can't he?"

"You got your answer," he said turning around on the stool, "So now I guess you are ready to pull your knife?"

He didn't, but he made it clear that he thought about it. He shouted that he was ready to die, and willing to take someone with him. Black men like him felt life was futile and that violence was both honorable and redemptive. The crowd with which street tough O.J. ran thought so too: "You'd hear cats saying: You gonna be at the Golden Gate Theater tomorrow? The Roman Gents are gonna fight the Sheiks." "Ba-ad," O.J. boasted: "I ran with a bunch of cutthroats."

In *Native Son*, Richard Wright effectively got into the minds of young men like street tough O.J. and showed how they displace their aggression. Bigger's pal Gus is plainly afraid of the consequences if he goes along with Bigger and robs and assaults a white man. When Gus rejects the idea, Bigger is enraged. He's really scared too, but he can't show it. Instead of robbing and assaulting the white man, he mercilessly pummels and kicks Gus while he's prone on the floor. The beating sends him into delirium: "Bigger laughed softly at first, then harder, louder, hysterically; feeling something like hot water bubbling inside of him trying to come out."

A modern day Bigger might have finished Gus off. He would have known how from watching TV. A white youth by age twelve has seen more than 40,000 murders or attempted murders and 250,000 violent acts on TV. Media critics have noted that TV crimes are likely to be more violent than real-life crime. Black youths by the same age will witness even more TV gore because they spend nearly twice as many hours in front of the tube. It's a short step for some to translate screen violence to street violence. O.J. often took that step. "I guess you try everything there is to try. Everything you see on TV."

The young O.J.s and the Biggers also perceive that society blocks them from achieving their social and professional goals and aspirations. This increases their frustration. O.J. realized this. "There are a lot of kids in the ghetto who remind me of what might have been if I hadn't gotten the opportunity and taken advantage of it." O.J. was no different from many poor, young blacks.

They intuitively know that the material goodies suspended before them in movies, on TV and in advertisements are the primary measures of an individual's worth in a consumerist and ultra-materialistic society. Young blacks want them, but they know that in many cases they won't attain them. This increases their frustration and anger. The American dream may be a dream deferred but it's still a dream that many spend their lives futiley reaching for.

The dream may not be enough for the black men who successfully claw their way out of poverty and attain the middle-class comforts. Pricey million dollar homes, country club memberships, a jet-set lifestyle, hefty bank accounts and a marriage to Nicole did not totally transform O.J. The internal rage still lay dangerously close to the surface. Anything, such as an insult, personal challenge, criticism or rejection, could trigger it.

In *Native Son*, Gus said, "Hi, how are you." That was enough. Bigger not only physically attacked him, he also pulled a knife and threatened to cut his throat. The violence escalated and became more deadly. The release of his pent up anger didn't calm him. It doesn't calm real instigators of violence either. The violence spirals and often results in serious injury or death.

• • • • • •

*B*lack women know this perhaps even better than young black males. It was gratifying to hear O.J.'s first wife, Marquerite, publicly state in an interview on ABC-TV's *20/20* before the start of the trial that O.J. did not physically abuse her during their marriage. But this was only one relationship. Physical and sexual abuse is a problem that many African-Americans must grapple with.

In November 1991, 1,603 black women, in response to the Hill-Thomas debacle, signed their names to a *New York Times* ad that read in part, "This country which has a long legacy of racism and sexism has never taken the sexual abuse of black women seriously. The common assumption in legal proceedings as well as in the larger society has been that black women can't be raped or otherwise sexually abused."

Although many of the women had some reservations about Hill's testimony, they were outraged at the way they felt the white male Senators on the Senate Judiciary Committee mistreated Hill. They were also angry at their treatment by society and by black men. Nation of Islam leader Louis Farrakhan sensed their pain. He urged his male followers to look at the part they play in "the destruction of the black home, the black family." The activist women who signed the ad almost certainly disagreed with the Nation of Islam's patriarchal position on women, yet they could applaud this.

Many black women have been victimized by black-male-directed violence. While young black males were killing each other, they were also killing and maiming black women. Between 1980 and 1985, the number of black women murdered exceeded the number of American soldiers killed in Vietnam in 1967, a peak year of the fighting. By 1990, homicide was the most common cause of death of young black females.

A black woman was ten times likelier to be raped than a white woman. She was four times likelier to be a homicide victim than a white woman. Black women often enter the same danger zone that black men like Gus, the man in *Invisible Man*, or O.J. would enter when they challenge black "manhood." Some black men view a woman as someone trying to control them, publicly upstaging them or manipulating them. They are angered and that anger can turn to violence.

• • • • • •

*S*exual abuse, like crime, is far from race neutral. White women are assaulted by white men and black women by black men. The media devalues both black and white women victims, but not in the same way. The media and society react with special fury to the infrequent times that black men attack white women. When black youths attacked a white woman in New York's Central Park in April 1989, the national media called the attack a "wilding" and ran hysterical stories for weeks.

There were fifty-four articles in the *New York Times* in April and May on the attack. Most of them were page one stories. The same month a fifteen-year-old black girl was brutally raped in East Harlem, and a black woman was raped and thrown off a building in Brooklyn. The *Times* ran two articles on the attacks in the back pages of the same edition.

The glorification of "gangsta" male toughness in books and music didn't help eliminate the double-standard in the treatment of black women. One rap group exhorted, "Scream when I put the safety pins in your nipples, hurt me, hurt me push it harder, shove it."

Black rappers are crucified by the media and much of the public. They are the targets of boycotts and angry editorials for these sexist and misanthropic lyrics. Country and Western and hard rock music are also loaded with sexist lyrics and both veiled and overt references to violence against women. Much of the media is mostly silent about that. And the rap groups that don't glorify male violence are largely ignored by the mainstream media.

The racial double standard is insulting, but there is a difference. Whites don't kill each other in disproportionate numbers and society doesn't tacitly minimize their deaths.

While young tough O.J. didn't kill anyone, he still remembered himself as a "gangsta" who could: "I was the Al Capone—I was the boss."

Blacks have no business trying to rationalize violence or abuse against females, and they should reject "urban survival syndrome" theories depicting black communities as urban jungles where violence is permissible as an ordinary means of survival. These theories are phony, self-serving, and allow a handful of young men to commit aggressive violence and get away with it.

With the eager help of some black filmmakers, Hollywood eagerly discovered black male aggression. During the 1970's and later in the 1990's, the movie screen was filled with an endless parade of pimps, hustlers, Superflys, Shafts, Sweetbacks and "boyz 'n the hood" "gangsta" types. When they weren't doing crime, they were whipping their women in line. Young whites had their drug store and midnight cowboys, Rambos, Terminators, Rockys, Missing in Action, and Under Assault types. But there were also films that depicted young whites coming of age, falling in love, discovering nature, and horsing around in slapstick comedy. Young whites weren't "gangstas" to the public. Young blacks were.

The media's depiction of Simpson as a clinically obsessed, sex-fiend was almost certainly an exaggeration. Yet O.J. didn't shy away from his image as a black macho superstud. He told *People* magazine in 1977, "Groupies would have been a problem in my youth, when I was insecure and needed to prove something." Young tough O.J. needed to prove it by fighting and brawling with other blacks on the streets of San Francisco. Celebrity O.J. proved it by his at times self-admitted fantasy of collecting and controlling women.

Celebrity superstar O.J. and street tough O.J. were in the same pathetic hunt for the perverse and distorted image of manhood that American society reserves for white men, and denies black men. Many black men kill and are killed for it. Many black women suffer and are killed because of it.

The men that commit these acts are victims of their warped reality. But so is society. Crime and violence can't be separated from the ills of American society. The terrorist carnage in Oklahoma City proved that. Victims and victimizers come in all colors, classes, and genders. But as long as many Americans are convinced that crime comes with a young black male face, they will continue to delude themselves that the key to their safety is a prison key.

## *five*
# The Hunt for Hidden Racism

*M*any whites and some blacks hotly denied that race was an issue in the O.J. Simpson case. It was easy for them to think that about the man an NBC executive described as "the single most popular employee" the network had. He could be called at home any time, night or day, and would be on a plane for an assignment. When O.J. played for the University of Southern California, it was practically a tradition for USC coaches and recruiters to bring prospective high school recruits over to O.J.'s locker after a game. He was never too tired to greet and encourage them.

In the pros, O.J. never spiked the football. He took his linemen out to dinner to show gratitude for their excellent blocking. Many star National Football League running backs now do the same thing. Often, the team bus would wait so that he could finish signing autographs for the fans. He regularly visited terminally ill children at Buffalo's hospitals quietly whispering words of cheer and encouragement to them.

He did not become just another burned out jock when his

playing days ended. He crafted a celebrity career as an actor, a media personality, and a businessman. From his earliest days at USC, O.J. was conscious and protective of his image as a football superstar and personality. He knew political controversy could diminish his professional market value. Racial controversy might end it. He made a special point to steer clear of the Black Student Union at USC. When black sprinters Tommie Smith and John Carlos gave their clenched fist Black Power salute on the victory stand at the 1968 Olympic Games in Mexico City, Simpson was asked his opinion. He was guarded: "I respect Tommie Smith but I don't admire him."

A USC student reporter pressed him to give his view of the threatened Olympic boycott by black athletes. O.J. gave what was probably his lengthiest public discourse on sports and black militancy. "I think they're going about the boycott the wrong way. You can't change the world until you change yourself. All this is going to do is make some Negro kid in high school football who isn't playing first string quit, saying, 'This guy isn't treating me right.'"

O.J. was the rarest of rare breeds, a black man who led a privileged life and was embraced by many whites. When he was arrested, a majority of whites backed him. Immediately after murder charges were filed, a *CNN* poll showed that nearly forty percent of whites still had "sympathy" for him. But that's only part of the reason for their "deracialization" of O.J.

● ● ● ● ● ●

$M$any whites believe that civil rights laws, court decisions, and affirmative action programs have expunged racism from America. This seems plausible on the surface. Whites walk into department stores and they see black managers. They sit next to blacks in corporate board meetings. They turn on the television and they see black reporters, commentators, and anchors. They leave their suburban homes and they see blacks living next door or across the street.

They take their children to exclusive private schools and they see black children arrive at the school in expensive cars and dressed in designer-label clothes. They live in cities that are run by black mayors where blacks are a majority on city councils, boards of education, and hold the top police and city department positions. They live in districts that are represented by black state or congressional representatives, or even a black senator.

Black progress is not an illusion in America. Some blacks have finally gotten a tiny piece of the pie. Seventy-five percent of blacks graduate from high school and thirty-two percent attend college. Since the 1970's, there has been a fifty-two percent increase in the number of black managers, professionals, technicians, and government officials.

Nearly one-third of blacks have incomes in excess of thirty-five thousand dollars and more than ten percent earn more than fifty thousand dollars annually. In 1994, the top 100 black businesses had gross sales of $11.71 billion. In O.J.'s home state, blacks are seven percent of the state population but hold an even greater percentage of white collar positions.

There's also an ugly side to the denial of racism. Many whites get angry or defensive when the issue of racism is raised, and blame blacks for always "making an issue out of race." They avoid having any physical or personal contact with blacks. They disassociate or change the subject when racial issues are brought up. They resist programs for ostensibly non-racial reasons; programs which they perceive as benefiting blacks or other people of color. They support organizations and leaders that promise to restore religion, moral values, and personal freedoms. They vote for candidates who promise to end the welfare state.

One example is the Republican "Contract with America." The supposedly anti-government, ultra-conservative-driven agenda would increase defense spending, cut education, wipe out many social programs, permanently kill national health care reform, and build more prisons. Republicans rammed some of the proposals through the House of Representatives in early 1995, and vowed to get the rest passed. There was no need for them to mention race in any of their legislation since it was already widely conceded that blacks and the poor would be hurt the most.

The more dangerous example of public racial denial is the militia and patriot movements. They depict themselves as "anti-government activists" fighting to preserve American freedoms. Their enemies are: the BATF, IRS, DEA, FBI, federal land agents, international bankers, the United Nations, and President Clinton. They exorcised derogatory references to blacks, Jews, Asians, Gays, and Feminists from their public statements and writings.

The con job worked. The media and some civil rights and civil liberties groups swallowed this sanitized pabulum. They claim that these groups are different from the old Klan, Nazi Party, and John Birch Society. They aren't. Their publications still read like a who's who of white supremacy and are crammed with the standard racist and Jew-baiting articles. They may differ on tactics, but they are united on three points: White Christians must rule America, the federal government is the enemy, and violence is the only accepted means to gain control.

It took a sensational double murder and a huge mass media launch to rocket O.J. into millions of American homes. That was not the case with the militias and patriots. They were already well-known before the Oklahoma City bombing. Neighbors heard militiamen detonating bombs on their land. Nothing was done. Local police knew that militias and patriots conducted mock military drills, parades, and exercises in their areas. Nothing was done. *Time* magazine did a feature story on the militias, and TV and radio stations interviewed their leaders. Nothing was done.

Military buddies, friends, relatives, and employers listened to accused bomber Timothy McVeigh spout violent, racist, anti-government rhetoric. Nothing was done. Millions of radio listeners heard convicted Watergate burglar and nationally syndicated talk show host, G. Gordon Liddy, advocate attacks on law enforcement and public officials. He received the Freedom of Speech award from the National Association of

Talk Show Hosts. A bevy of other hate talk jocks followed his lead and regularly took verbal shots at "government tyranny." Nothing was done. There was little public demand for a federal probe of rightist hate groups. The O.J. trial returned as the front page news story as well as the major subject at America's dinner tables.

Now suppose that groups of blacks or Arab-Americans used the Internet, short-wave broadcasts, and publications to send hate-filled messages, gain recruits, and solicit funds. Suppose they advocated, organized, and committed attacks against the FBI, BATF, and IRS agents and pulled off bank robberies. Suppose they told millions of listeners to take head shots at federal agents. Suppose they exploded bombs, stock-piled munitions, and paraded around in camouflage fatigues. And sadly, suppose a black or Arab-American had been accused of committing the greatest domestic mass murder attack in American history. How would America have reacted?

One need look no further than O.J. Once the media hoopla was stripped away, the O.J. case was still basically a murder case. The criminal justice system handles dozens of them every day. But when the media tossed in wealth, power, sports stardom, and celebrity status to the case, and topped it off with the public's hate-fascination with racial and sexual stereotypes, the militias, and patriots quickly faded as contenders to replace O.J. as America's latest obsession.

• • • • • •

*T*he manufacture of race, sex, and class scapegoats depends heavily on self-serving myths. Republican Congressman Newt Gingrich got right to it: "When you hear gunshots in your nation's capitol at night and you know that young Americans have died needlessly, then we have every reason to have the moral courage to confront every weakness of the current structure and replace it." He managed to pack all the racial stereotypes and code words into one sentence: crime in the streets, violent young black males, moral decay, liberal permissiveness, the bankruptcy of social programs, and conservative resuscitation.

Gingrich had the myth mill humming well. He wasn't alone. Many whites (and some blacks) busily repeated the same racial myths that have been prevalent for the past century.

*Myth:* Blacks have worse jobs, less income, and poorer housing than whites because they just don't have the motivation or will power to pull themselves up out of poverty. In 1991, fifty-seven percent of whites believed this.

*Fact:* Mrs. Eunice Simpson, O.J.'s mother, raised four children, lived in a housing project, and worked two jobs. She was not an exception. Blacks have worked steadier and longer than whites during most of the twentieth century. The labor force participation of black males has always mirrored and at times exceeded that of white males. The labor force participation of black females has always been far greater than that of white females.

The only real gap is among teenagers: 55.8 percent of whites and 35.4 percent of blacks were employed during the 1980's. This has nothing to do with lack of motivation, low self-esteem, or personal irresponsibility on the part of young blacks. It has everything to do with lack of skills, education, resources, transportation, job training, networking connections, and most importantly racism.

In Chicago, a significant number of employers ranked blacks last (Hispanics were a distant second) on work ethics. They called them lazy, dishonest, and ignorant. Many flatly said they used every tactic from refusing to take applications to denying applicant's interviews to evade fair employment laws. Blacks were caught in a vicious Catch-22. With the chronic high unemployment rate in black communities, many blacks desperately needed work, yet many private employers believed the myths, considered them damaged goods, and refused to hire them. The official unemployment rate for black males continued to hover at double and triple the rate for white males.

*Myth:* Blacks are lazier and prefer welfare to working. In 1990, sixty-two percent of whites thought the former, and a whopping seventy-eight percent thought the latter.

*Fact and Commentary:* "My mother was never on welfare." This was always a special point of pride for O.J. But even if Mrs. Simpson had been, she would still have been among only a small minority of black women that exist on welfare. The example of Mrs. Simpson, notwithstanding, many Americans still believe the opposite.

At an American Jewish Committee breakfast in March 1994, the topic shifted to the problems of the black community. Martin Peretz, *New Republic* magazine editor-in-chief, was the featured speaker. With no apparent sense of impropriety, Peretz said, "So many people in the black population are afflicted by deficiencies." He didn't back away when mildly challenged by then Chairman of the Congressional Black Caucus, Democratic Congressman Kwesi Mfume. He added, "In the ghetto—a lot of mothers don't appreciate the importance of schooling, and are threatened by their children."

It was a lie. Nearly two out of three welfare recipients are non-black. Whites are the majority of that total. They stay on welfare on average less than four years. If jobs and child care are available they take them. Mrs. Eunice Simpson worked steadily, put her kids through school, while managing to keep them out of trouble. Much of the time, as O.J. said, she got help from her estranged husband, Jimmy, O.J.'s father.

Many editors and publishers of major publications apparently agreed with Peretz. *Nation* magazine columnist Alexander Cockburn called and faxed Peretz's statements to the editors at the *New Yorker*, the *New York Times Magazine*, the *Washington Monthly*, *Newsweek*, *Vanity Fair*, the *Partisan Review*, *Jewish Forward* and the *National Catholic Reporter*. He deliberately chose publications that spanned the opinion spectrum from conservative to liberal.

Not one of the publications that bothered to respond condemned Peretz. O.J. answered their silence with the example of his mother and her children. Mrs. Simpson, he reiterated, was "a working lady" that "fended for herself." Her children, likewise, were "doing for themselves."

• • • • • •

*The Ultimate Myth:* After his arrest, there were snide hints from "unnamed sources" in media articles and features that O.J. got as far as he did in college and the corporate world because of his sports fame, luck, opportunism, and the ability to manipulate; not by his intelligence and professional skill. This fit neatly into the age-old notion that blacks are inherently intellectually inferior to whites.

In 1994, Richard Herrnstein and Charles Murray published *The Bell Curve.* They claimed that America's racial ills were intractable largely because many blacks (and the poor of all races) were genetically intellectually deficient. The pair would have been laughed at and dismissed as hucksters a few years ago. In 1994, they weren't. Murray (Herrnstein died) appeared on countless talk shows and had *carte blanche* to defend his ideas. The book went through seven printings in a month and hovered near the top of the best seller lists.

Many whites didn't need to read *The Bell Curve* to be convinced that blacks were intellectually inferior. In 1990, fifty-three percent of whites told National Opinion Research Center interviewers that they believed blacks were less intelligent than whites. A majority of whites in supposedly cosmopolitan New York and Los Angeles said that blacks were stupider. In the last decade opinion polls confirm that many whites believe blacks are lazy, crime-prone and intellectually deficient.

*The Bell Curve* was timely and rested on three basic points that seemed plausible on the surface:

- IQ tests are valid measures of intelligence;
- Some percentage of intelligence is hereditary; and
- IQ tests predict success in life.

*Fact*: There is no precise definition of intelligence. Psychologists have identified seven different creative/intellectual processes that require cognitive thought. There may be even more. It would be impossible to design a test to measure them all. Many geneticists contend that genes are significant as markers, not determiners, of an individual's intellectual capacity. Even this is speculative. Geneticists do not know precisely how they influence behavior. Most agree that genes do interact with the environment to shape the learning process in an individual. Teachers are more likely to track, guide, motivate, and reinforce more alert students.

IQ tests reflect the cultural influences, environmental conditioning, and educational opportunity, more than cognitive ability. The standardized IQ scores measure a student's knowledge and mastery of vocabulary, reading skills, geometric angles, and mathematical principles. Few inner city schools are equipped with state-of-the-art math labs, computers and calculators, design materials, the latest edition math textbooks and tutors, or can afford reading comprehension specialists. It would take that and much more to effectively level the IQ playing field.

Murray and Herrnstein contended that IQ correlates with professional and business success. There is no evidence that college grade point average correlates with occupational success in business, engineering, medicine, law, and science. Murray would be hard-pressed to take an individual's IQ score and predict whether that person would be an outstanding professional achiever or a mediocre one.

Murray, however, vehemently denied that he was a racist. Whether that was true or not is immaterial. He and Herrnstein mangled science and gave academic validation to the worst racial stereotype—black genetic inferiority.

The IQ controversy, as well as black poverty and crime, are issues only because many Americans see blacks not as equals but as grotesque caricatures to be tolerated, humored, and patronized. In 1968, the *Daily Trojan* had this to say about the school's budding football superstar: "His environment shows through in the grammatical inconsistencies in his deep, rumbling speech, but he absorbs and understands as well as any man." The *Daily Trojan* apparently didn't measure O.J.'s IQ. Yet it still seemed amazed that he could think "as well as any man."

• • • • • •

While much of the media and the prosecution worked overtime to minimize race in the Simpson case, it was still there. I'll compare two cases—Jeffrey Dahmer and O.J. Simpson. In 1991, Dahmer admitted that he sexually savaged, mutilated, and hacked up seventeen mostly black, Asian, Latino, and gay males. O.J. denied that he committed murder.

I examined the August 5, and 12, 1991 issues of *Time* following Dahmer's confession and the June 27, and July 4, 1994 issues of *Time* following O.J.'s plea of not guilty. I chose *Time* because it is considered the authoritative standard for American journalism. When black men are charged with crimes the media often presume guilt, pander to sensationalism, and promote racial stereotypes. Did *Time* do that?

***Racial Stereotyping:*** *Time,* after many protests from blacks, admitted that it doctored O.J.'s cover photo to make him look more sinister. When blacks protested, managing editor James R. Gains at first blamed the distorted photo on a freelance artist commissioned by the magazine. This explanation satisfied no one.

Several black journalists confronted Gains at a conference co-sponsored by the National Association of Black Journalists in Atlanta in 1994. They called the distorted cover "a racist act." Gains backed away—slightly. He denied that any "racial implication was intended." He insisted that it was an editorial decision that newspapers and magazines make all the time. They routinely crop, touch-up, and retouch the pictures of politicians, personalities, and even presidents for satirical or caricature affect.

The *Time* cover was not satire. There were no space considerations on the cover. There were no artistic reasons to create a different mood. *Time* did not tamper with two pictures of Dahmer. He is shown as a sad-eyed, contrite young man. (Nor did *Time* touch up its cover photo of Ollie North or executed serial killer John Wayne Gacy.) The *Time* mug shot of O.J. fit into the historic pattern of covert media bias.

***Presumption of Guilt:*** *Time* seemed bewildered about Dahmer. It asked, "How can it have happened?" It didn't dissect his personality or make judgments about his character. It simply quoted his stepmother who called him "sick" and an FBI agent who called him "dysfunctional."

Transcripts of police calls showed that officers ignored the complaints of black residents about the violence and returned a fleeing victim to Dahmer. The police left after inspecting his apartment. Although three officers were suspended, *Time* cautiously noted that the police "apparently badly blundered."

While *Time* railed against "promiscuous speculation" about O.J., it called his relationship with Nicole "dangerous" and "dysfunctional." It did not criticize L.A. County District Attorney Gil Garcetti's early media trial of O.J. In a companion article on Nicole it asked, "Is it her fault she's dead." The implication was that her murder was the direct result of the couple's well-publicized domestic conflicts.

The article blamed both the prosecution and the defense for "playing to the crowd" to "win" sympathy. Yet it leveled the heaviest attack against the defense. This created the impression that O.J. needed sympathy because he's guilty.

When Dahmer was sentenced to fifteen life-sentences, neither *Time* nor the prosecutors mentioned the death penalty. In O.J.'s case, though the initial evidence was circumstantial and contested, *Time* more than once noted that prosecutors might ask for the death penalty. Incredibly, Dahmer's bail was set at $1 million. There was no bail for O.J.

**Sensationalism:** *Time* called Dahmer's thirteen-year orgy of barbarism, a "murderous rampage." It called O.J. a "suicidal fugitive." It termed the case the "most publicly shocking crime in years" and a "howling, monstrous tragedy." It called the murders "savagery" and the "precis of butchery."

O.J. was not arrested and did not stand trial because he was black. The era of lynch mobs, fiery crosses, "whites-only" signs, race-baiting Southern political demagogues, and legally segregated schools are nearly a thing of the past. Many blacks have prospered and attained middle-class comforts.

O.J. symbolized how much some blacks have succeeded. He confirmed for many whites and some blacks that America had become a race-neutral society where only performance not color count.

But the great IQ debate about blacks and the casual acceptance by much of the media and the public of racial stereotypes are signs that racism has not been expunged from American life. It has changed form. The collective denial of race has replaced racial compassion.

Shortly before his trial began, O.J. finally faced the naked truth that his wealth and fame only partially shielded him from racial bias. In a jailhouse interview, he admitted that "he believed racism is a part of his trial." When he entered the courtroom, he said that he counted the number of blacks, Hispanics and Asians in the room. He claimed that this was the first time in many years that race really mattered to him.

It is hardly a first for other African-Americans. Until many Americans stop believing, and politicians and business leaders stop creating public policy and law based on racial stereotypes, African-Americans will continue to be victimized by them. Even O.J.

## six
# Conspiracy or Collective Paranoia?

*A* week after O.J. was arrested, Nation of Islam leader Louis Farrakhan warned that the media "destroyed" him. He fingered *Time* magazine for doctoring the cover picture of O.J. to make him look sinister and menacing. Farrakhan claimed that *Time* "did the same to me" in a cover picture.

Nearly every African-American I talked to before and during the trial asked, "Do you think O.J. did it?" Before I could answer, the questioner snapped, "Well, I don't think he did it." When I asked how did they know, they repeated the standard mush of rumor, innuendo, gossip, half-truth, and fluff. Almost always it boiled down to: "They're out to get the brother."

When I tentatively suggested that the circumstantial evidence against him was still evidence, they retorted, "He was framed." When I asked by whom, the list of "conspirators" included: The Mafia, Columbian drug dealers, Las Vegas gamblers, the LAPD, the Los Angeles County District Attorney, the Klan, the caretaker, and even O.J.'s son.

When *Newsweek* asked blacks the same question, some simply said "by persons unknown." When I asked them why anyone would want to frame him, they said he was into cocaine; he had big gambling debts; he was an uppity black man; he was married to a white woman; or he was having extramarital affairs with white women.

*CNN* polls in July and August 1994 repeatedly found that whites believed the case against O.J. was strong. Forty-five percent of blacks disagreed. The majority of whites said that he would get a fair trial. The majority of blacks said that he wouldn't. The case flung many blacks and whites to separate planets that were in no danger of colliding. O.J. would have been the last one I'd have picked to harden racial lines and unleash paranoia. O.J. along with Bill Cosby and Colin Powell are the only three black men, who weren't exclusively entertainers, since Booker T. Washington, to appear to have gained widespread acceptance by middle-class Americans.

O.J. was not Cosby or Powell. Cosby gave substantial sums to black colleges, made frequent fundraising and charity appearances for black causes, and refused to play demeaning, stereotyped roles. He often criticized discriminatory hiring practices in Hollywood and the broadcast media.

Powell at times cut through the spit and polish of the dedicated my-country-right-or-wrong general, and praised the accomplishments and heroism of black soldiers who served when the American military was segregated. He acknowledged that racism was still a powerful force in American life and told young blacks, "Let it be a problem to some one else."

He quickly accepted the offer to be the Grand Marshall of the annual Martin Luther King Day parade in Atlanta in 1991. Many blacks were pleased that Powell "was in touch with his blackness."

O.J. rarely publicly commented on racial matters. When he did, his remarks were cautious, tepid, guarded, and calculated to reassure the public that racial problems were at worst a minor annoyance. Yet he still bucked the ground-rules that blacks traditionally use to pick their martyrs:

- A black group or individual had to be under attack by the "white establishment" for resisting injustice. The examples are legion. They include: civil rights activists, Black Panthers, defrocked politicians, religious leaders, athletes blackballed from their sport or slandered by sportswriters, managers or owners, and outspoken entertainers.

- An African-American whose house was bombed by racists, or who was beaten, or killed by the Klan, Aryan Nation, Skinheads, Nazis, or the police. Rodney King was hardly the first to trigger a racial explosion. The examples are equally legion.

- A prominent black in a high-profile case who appears to have been punished more severely than a prominent white who committed the same crime. The best example is still Mike Tyson vs. William Kennedy Smith.

O.J. didn't fit any of these examples. Yet the knees of many blacks still jerked for him as they did for any African-American in the court docket. There are reasons. Many blacks remember the savage history of lynchings, shootings, burnings, and beatings. They still see laws enforced by white police, judges, prosecutors, and juries. They still see a disproportionate number of black men being arrested and sentenced to stiff prison terms and the death penalty. They believe that the system is the inherent enemy of African-Americans.

When much of the media tossed the presumption of innocence out the window with O.J., many blacks were convinced that white society would automatically judge, try, and convict black men accused of crimes even before a jury could bring in a verdict.

Many blacks feel hopelessly entrapped by race. No sane person would judge the character of white males by convicted mass murderer Jeffrey Dahmer. But when a black is accused of or commits a crime, blacks perceive that the entire race is on trial. That's because many Americans seldom make formal gender, class, political, or religious distinctions between blacks. Malcolm X once told a black audience, "you're all a nigger, you're all in the same boat." For many blacks this was more than just hyperbole or a throw away line.

● ● ● ● ● ●

*M*any blacks regarded O.J. as only the latest smear target. The Nation of Islam warned that sinister plots, secret relationships, hidden agendas, and covert plans were being hatched to destabilize black organizations and wipe out black leaders.

Many African-Americans agreed. It was now respectable, even fashionable to talk about conspiracies and plots against blacks.

On nearly every radio talk show I appeared on in 1994 and 1995, the host asked, "Do you think there's a conspiracy against blacks?" Many African-American telephone callers on these shows dutifully named an assorted list of plotters that ran the gamut from international Zionists to the CIA.

The O.J. case brought the conspiracy fears of African-Americans exploding to the surface precisely because he didn't visibly identify with black causes. He moved easily in the corporate world of money and power. His friends and personal relations were mostly white. If the mainstream media could relentlessly assault his character and prosecutors could orchestrate a damaging campaign to convince the public of his guilt even before a trial, then every black was fair game. This would provide yet another excuse to marginalize, repress, and eventually physically eliminate blacks.

O.J., the conspiracy theorists believed, was a link in a racial plot that began following the urban civil disturbances of the mid-1960's. The ghettos were flooded with drugs, alcohol, gangs, and guns to turn militancy inward and get blacks to self-destruct.

During the 1980's, AIDS was imported into the inner cities by "sinister" government forces to wipe out blacks. Many gays charged that AIDS was part of a conspiracy to wipe them out, too. Many blacks compared it to the forty-year Tuskeegee experiments that began in the 1930's in which the government withheld penicillin from 399 black men stricken with syphilis. The "white establishment" wanted to stop blacks from developing unity, strong political organizations, and programs to counter oppression.

Farrakhan specifically named the "unseen forces" behind the plot. "Where do the drugs come from? Who is the unseen hand? The government of the United States." In editorials and articles in 1994, the Nation of Islam's newspaper, *The Final Call*, raged that the "unseen forces" had a global master plan to plunder Africa's strategic minerals and annihilate African-American leaders. The headlines read, "America's Secret War Against Blacks," "Is Ben Chavis Being Set Up," "The Plot to Control Our Bodies," and "The Plan to Destroy Our Race."

● ● ● ● ● ●

*T*here is no hard evidence that a small group of white plotters in the secret chambers of government or corporate boardrooms move and manipulate people and events around like pieces on a chessboard. Yet many blacks are conditioned to see a hidden racial hand behind every catastrophe. They refuse to believe that race is not central to every issue. They, along with much of the media, are in a frantic rush to make the public believe that everything in America is a perennial crisis in black and white.

The O.J. case was typical. *Newsweek* called it a symptom of the deepening "racial divide over Simpson's guilt or innocence." The media played the race card this way. Whites believed he was guilty. Blacks believed he was innocent. Whites insisted that the system was not unfair and that he wasn't framed. Blacks said that he was. If sports or media personalities John Madden, Frank Gifford, or Joe Montana had been accused of the crime, the prosecution and media would have treated them the same way they treated O.J.

In August 1994, *Newsweek* published the results of several polls to prove that the racial divide existed. They asked blacks and whites, "Was O.J. framed?" *Newsweek* was appalled that a "staggering" sixty percent of blacks agreed. What was so staggering about that? Sixty percent was hardly an overwhelming majority, nor did it represent a consensus of opinion about the case.

During the middle of the trial, *Newsweek* asked blacks and whites again about O.J.'s guilt. This time fifty-six percent of blacks thought he was not guilty. *Newsweek* once more declared that blacks and whites were oceans apart in their view of Simpson's guilt. But fifty-six percent hardly indicated anything approaching unanimity on his innocence.

The polls were less a referendum among blacks on O.J.'s guilt than on the criminal justice system. Many did not believe that an African-American, even a wealthy and famous celebrity like O.J., could get a fair trial. This did not mean that they believed that he was incapable of committing murder.

Also, twenty-one percent of whites also agreed that he was framed. That figure was more significant. One in five whites resisted the onslaught of media condemnation and innuendoes about O.J.'s guilt and believed that he was innocent. *Newsweek* asked whether O.J. was treated the same as a white murder suspect. Thirty-eight percent of whites and forty percent of blacks agreed. This was also significant.

Nearly as many whites as blacks perceived that a wealthy, famous African-American received no better treatment than a white of any income or class status. They did not react in a Pavlovian-like manner to the racial stereotypes about black men and white women. They didn't try and convict him for the murder before the trial.

This is not unusual. During the past century many whites have been prepared to give black men the benefit of the doubt when they were charged with crimes. Many have stood up to lynch mobs and Southern sheriffs. They have also defied segregation laws, bankrolled black organizations, and supported black leaders and political candidates. Robert Shapiro, a white attorney, stood behind O.J. from the very start. He believed in his innocence and fought to prove it.

In *Native Son*, Max, a white attorney, represented Bigger Thomas on trial for murdering a white woman. Bigger, unlike O.J., distrusts all whites. He tells his white attorney, Max, "They hate black folks." Max retorts "Bigger, I know my face is white. But I want you to know that you can trust me." He could. Max believed in fairness and risked the wrath of public opinion to defend a black man accused of the ultimate crime.

Much of the media attributed O.J.'s popularity among whites to his status as a deracialized black sports icon and corporate pitch man in a society pretending to be color-free. There was another possible explanation. America remains a racially-diverse nation. Almost certainly many whites admired him as a African-American who overcame poverty and discrimination, and who achieved success. Perhaps many whites implicitly recognized that he and other blacks should be allowed to attain the American dream without sacrificing racial identity or pretending that racism doesn't exist.

O.J. recognized that. During a golfing match at the exclusive Rockland Country Club in New York, he told an interviewer, "There's no excuse for golf courses near major cities not to have black members. But I know it's the case."

● ● ● ● ● ●

$M$ost whites and some blacks laughed at, ridiculed, and lampooned blacks who charged that hidden conspiracies were behind everything. Still, there is the old line that even paranoiacs have enemies. Americans have always had a special affinity for a paranoid style in times of crisis.

Malcolm X was partially right when he charged that there was a "government conspiracy" to deny blacks their rights. The conspiracy wasn't to deny rights. It was to spy and disrupt black organizations and discredit black leadership. FBI Director J. Edgar Hoover had a near-clinical obsession with "preventing the rise of a black Messiah." He used the FBI's entire arsenal of dirty tricks from poison pen letters to murderous police raids to hammer Malcolm X, Martin Luther King, and the Black Panther Party.

If private individuals or organizations had engaged in the illegal practices that the government engaged in against black organizations, the public would have laughed at the lunacy and their perpetrators would have been indicted. But they weren't private groups. They were the U.S. military and the federal government. Decades of government spying indulged the paranoid delusions of a national security state, cost taxpayers millions, violated civil liberties, and chilled legitimate dissent.

O.J. was not a political prisoner or a victim of government-initiated persecution for his political views or activities. There was no public record that he ever said anything that could be considered even remotely controversial about the government or the media establishment. He never took part in any militant protest actions that would have made him a political target. O.J., after his jailing, protested that the same government that spied on black organizations had violated his constitutional rights and unjustly incarcerated him for crimes he didn't commit. He was blunt: "I don't believe in the legal system anymore."

O.J. had a short memory. In 1989, he was charged with battering Nicole. He received no jail time, a token fine, and was required to undergo a few weeks of counseling. The legal system that he no longer trusted bent over backward at the time to protect him. Two police officers came to the house the night of the "incident" to investigate. They left when he told them "It was nothing."

The media establishment quickly closed ranks around him. It took a month for the newspapers to report the arrest. Even that was too much for O.J. "I was stunned that it made the papers." NBC held a news conference in July. Simpson was there. The arrest was never even mentioned. A week after the press conference, a curious reporter asked O.J. about the arrest. He treated it as a joke and laughingly told Nicole, "Hey Nicole, this is the guy who reminded the public about our little spat on New Years."

Much, of course, had happened in the five years between his arrest for the murder of Nicole Simpson and Ron Goldman and the domestic violence charge. There was the Rodney King beating, the failure of a jury with no blacks to convict the LAPD officers of the beating, the civil disturbances in Los Angeles and nationwide, widespread reports of police abuse of minorities, the disproportionate arrests of young black males, and the reports of LAPD spying on prominent local blacks.

Then there was the Simpson defense team's allegation that LAPD detective Mark Fuhrman hated blacks, and had planted incriminating evidence at O.J.'s estate. This supposedly was part of an elaborate LAPD conspiracy to frame O.J. The defense and O.J. may have been grasping at straws in a desperate ploy to win an acquittal. Despite Fuhrman's audio tape "role play" confessional that some LAPD officers abused blacks, it defied credulity to believe that the LAPD had the resources, skill, or even the motive to frame O.J. It would have been a monumental task for the LAPD to pull it off. But that wasn't the point. Many blacks thought the police could and did. More importantly, one of those who did was O.J.

•  •  •  •  •  •

*T*o further bolster their case that prominent blacks like O.J.

were under special attack by the government, the conspiracy theorists and believers cited the treatment of black elected officials. In recent years they have been especially inviting targets. Their growing numbers pose a potential challenge to the political patronage and control of old guard Democrats and Republicans. They also might provide new political direction for the black poor.

Between 1983 and 1988, the Reagan Justice Department initiated 465 political corruption probes of elected officials. Fourteen percent of the investigations were against black elected officials even though they comprised only three percent of U.S. elected officials.

From 1981 to 1993, half of the twenty-six members of the Congressional Black Caucus were subjects of federal investigations. To put the magnitude of the investigations in perspective, this is equivalent to bringing charges against 204 of the 409 white Congressional representatives. An FBI agent admitted, "The purpose of the policy was the routine investigation of prominent black elected and appointed officials throughout the United States." It was more than that. Republican Attorney Generals Edwin Meese and Richard Thornburgh insisted that the probes were intended to ferret out political corruption and not to harass black elected officials.

Were they telling the truth? Yes and no. Taking money for political favors is a time-honored tradition in American politics. FBI and Justice Department investigators have caught many white elected officials in pay-off stings. In 1994, the FBI trapped twelve elected state officials in California in bribe-taking and influence-peddling scams. They were indicted, convicted, and imprisoned. Some were Republicans. Many were influential. All were white.

Undoubtedly, partisan politics was mixed in. Most of those prosecuted nationally were Democrats and most of the prosecutors were Reagan-appointed conservative Republicans. The Democratic officeholders who took bribes and political favors were easy prey for two unabashedly partisan Republican Attorney Generals Meese and Thornburgh. In the end, the bribe-taking politicians were victims of their own greed, not race. Some U.S. attorneys sincerely believed that there was solid evidence that some black elected officials were also taking bribes for political favors.

Even though most of the black House Democrats indicted and tried were acquitted, there are far fewer black elected officials than whites. It was not inconceivable that some Reaganite officials calculated that investigating black and white elected officials would have a more damaging impact on blacks. This would have created divisions, suspicions, and blunted the political effectiveness of black elected officials.

They may have anticipated that the press would apply its customary racial double-standard of saturating the public with sensationalist features and exposes of high-profile blacks accused of, or suspected of, committing crimes. That was true with Marion Barry, Mike Tyson, and the much maligned boxing promoter Don King. Media mania and sensationalism reached its maddening zenith with O.J.

None of this should excuse black criminal wrongdoing.

Black politicians have a special duty to the black community. Many blacks view them not as politicians, but leaders and advocates. They look to them to represent their interests and to challenge and confront institutional power. When they take bribes, they betray the trust of African-Americans. They should not be treated as folk heroes persecuted by the white establishment, but as crooks.

• • • • • •

*T*o accuse much of the media and witch-hunting government officials of applying racial double-standards is not the same as condoning criminal behavior. This is an important distinction that many blacks refuse to make. They forget that the press would not eagerly malign black politicians and prominent personalities if they hadn't committed crimes or there was strong evidence that they had.

Many blacks failed to make that distinction in the case of Joseph Jett. For three months Jett was the talk of Wall Street and the media. The chief government bond trader for Kidder, Peabody for two years, had worked a scam that netted the firm $350 million in paper profits. Jett rigged purchases and trades, and manipulated the markets. In April 1994, Kidder blew the whistle after the SEC began investigating. Jett was fired. Firm executives reacted with shock, anger, and disbelief. The parent company, General Electric, promised to investigate. Kidder officials promised to fully cooperate.

Jett's defense was predictable. He screamed racism. He

claimed senior executives made him a "scapegoat" to cover their crimes and that they had full knowledge of and approved the crooked deals. Did Jett have a point? Was it racism? Or was it criminality? The greed of Wall Street is legendary. The Securities Exchange Commission probes of Wall Street trading practices and the occasional indictments of brokers during the 1980's are well known.

Most analysts agreed that Jett could not have perpetuated such a massive fraud under the noses of Kidder executives for two years without higher-ups knowing about it. Jett, however, was not an unwilling pawn. He knew what he was doing and he profited handsomely. He had two years to say no. He would not have been the first employee of a company who refused to go along with criminality. If they were crooks, so was Jett. His color could not excuse or change that. The same standard applied to O.J. If he was indeed guilty, his color should not excuse or change that for him either.

Blacks are justified in suspecting that government agencies occasionally play fast and loose with the rules of democracy in their overzealous search for political enemies. There were signs that O.J. was a victim of dirty tricks. The tactics engaged in by much of the press such as leaks, sensationalism, rumor and gossip, not to mention the possible tainting of evidence by the prosecution before his trial, could have been pages torn straight from Hoover's sordid play book.

Still it is dangerous and counterproductive for blacks to circle the wagons, mistake friends for enemies, defend, or make excuses for blacks who commit crimes, and find enemies under every bedpost. There was no government conspiracy or secret plot to get O.J. or other prominent blacks. Sadly, the ugly mix of past repression and paranoia is the reason many blacks believed there was.

# seven

# The Delusion of the Sports Icon

"*I* couldn't sing or dance, and I wasn't going to be a brain surgeon. So it had to be sports." There was no middle ground for the fourteen-year-old O.J. Simpson. It was sports or nothing. For a time it appeared that O.J. was destined to be another monument to ghetto failure. But then something happened. "Wherever I went people were talking about Willie Mays. I realized that this was a black guy they were talking about and that it didn't matter." Willie Mays paid a visit to his home and spent a day with him. "Mays made me realize my dream was possible." It was. It also planted the illusion that race could be buried under fan idolatry. Mays probably knew better.

During Mays's years in baseball, he carefully avoided racial or political controversy. This won him the adulation of fans and sportswriters. But shortly after he was inducted into the Baseball Hall of Fame, baseball commissioner Bowie Kuhn summarily banned him from baseball. He claimed Mays sullied the "image" of baseball by accepting a public relations job at Bally's Casino in Atlantic City.

Kuhn ignored Mays's protest that the sport was hypocritical. Some baseball owners gambled, owned, and played the horses. He pointed out to Kuhn that New Jersey law forbade casino employees from entering the gaming rooms. But Mays was not Pete Rose. Rose bet on his team, the Cincinnati Reds, consorted with known gamblers and loan sharks, and evaded federal taxes. He finally admitted that he had a gambling problem. He was convicted of tax evasion, slapped with a five-year federal prison sentence, and banned from baseball.

However, when Rose was disqualified from Baseball's Hall of Fame in 1991, baseball fans and sportswriters were enraged. "The Rose case," *New York Times* sports columnist Ira Berkow wrote, "has touched the emotions of a surprisingly large number of people." Berkow, fans, and sportswriters roundly criticized Commissioner Fay Vincent and the judges who voted to disqualify him. In contrast, fans and sportswriters didn't rush to bat for Mays. It took several years, a new baseball commissioner, and a properly ingratiating Mays before the ban was lifted.

Although Arthur Ashe attained fame in the country club sport of tennis, he did not delude himself that fan adoration meant racial acceptance. Immediately after he publicly disclosed in 1992 that he had AIDS, a reporter for *People* magazine asked him:

"Mr. Ashe, I guess this must be the heaviest burden you have ever had to bear?"

Ashe didn't hesitate:

"You're not going to believe this, but being black is the greatest burden I've had to bear. Even now it continues to feel like an extra weight tied around me."

Ashe tried to loosen the weight. He protested discrimination. He was arrested at demonstrations against South African apartheid. He criticized the Bush administration policies denying refugee status to Haitians. He lectured on black college campuses. He wrote articles on discrimination in sports. He was troubled by the slavish adulation of athletes by many young blacks. He felt their importance to the black community was vastly overrated. During visits to black high schools, he was thunderstruck by "the obsession with sports that borders on pathology."

Ashe understood that society was ultimately to blame for transforming superstar athletes into demigods. He offered the example of his life as a way to reshape their one-dimensional image of athletes. Ashe felt it was important that young blacks see that some athletes were making contributions outside the sportsworld. He had a choice to teach at prestigious Yale or tiny Florida Memorial College, a historically black college. He spent a year at the latter. He explained why: "There are lots of things that people need to know and have impressed upon them."

Mays also recognized that young impressionable black youth like O.J. idolized superstar athletes: "Kids are affected by their sports heroes and someone in my position could make a difference."

• • • • • •

Sports heroes aren't the only ones who can make a difference. O.J. realized that there was life beyond the playing field. A week after he won the Heisman Trophy in 1968, he told a reporter that he wanted to work with juveniles in San Francisco when his playing career ended. "A lot of people who make good should go back and work in their community."

This was implicit recognition that others had shaped his success. His father, Jimmy Simpson, was one. The press in the chase for tabloid sensationalism spun not one, not two, but three popular racial stereotypes out of the elder Simpson's alleged non-relationship with O.J.

- Stereotype #1: Jimmy was a devil-may-care, chronic loser who abandoned his family when O.J. was five (derelict, irresponsible).
- Stereotype #2: Jimmy was a homosexual, possibly a transvestite, "a potential source of shame," *Newsweek* assured, "to a black youth growing up" (sexual menace).
- Stereotype #3: Jimmy was a tyrant, possible wife beater and child abuser (savage, brute).

This was pure media concoction. Neither O.J., his mother, his sisters, nor his brother drew this composite picture of Jimmy Simpson. None of them publicly criticized his lifestyle or the way he treated his family. O.J. remembered Jimmy differently: "Even though my dad didn't live under the same roof as us during most of my youth, he was always there anytime I had a problem. I love you for it Dad."

Significantly, O.J. made this public declaration about his father during his acceptance speech when he was inducted into the Pro Football Hall of Fame at Canton, Ohio in 1985. Jimmy had never stopped playing a part as O.J.'s disciplinarian, authority figure, and role model.

Mays was not star-struck by celebrity-athletes either. A reporter once asked him if Jackie Robinson was his hero. Mays was properly respectful and appreciative of Robinson's contribution, but he was not his hero. "My father was my idol."

The media was much gentler with O.J.'s mom. She fit the popularly accepted, benevolent stereotype of the hard-working, long-suffering black woman battling against the odds to raise her children without a man in the home. They acknowledged that she was a role model for him. It was hard not to. O.J. listed his life guides as "my mother, the Bible, and do unto others."

Many black athletes traditionally praise and credit their mothers. Mrs. Simpson was an easy concession. Her real strength was in her determination to make sure that O.J. succeeded off the playing field. In his Canton speech, appropriately he publicly thanked her for working two jobs, taking the family on vacations, and being a tough disciplinarian.

O.J. had role models among his friends. They weren't endowed with his incredible athletic talent. Probably few could sing, dance, or become brain surgeons. Some of them surely found their way out of the ghetto even without a visit from Mays. Al Cowlings did. A neighborhood gang rival, he and O.J. soon became close friends. Cowlings, as did O.J., also shed the tough-guy image. A friend, impressed with his compassion and gentle demeanor, remarked, "A.C. is the nicest person. When you're in the room with him, nice gets all over you."

Sports was his ticket out of the ghetto. He won a football scholarship to USC, where he made honorable mention on several All-American teams. But Cowlings was not O.J. He was a journeyman lineman in the pros. There were stints with the Buffalo Bills, Houston Oilers, Seattle Seahawks, and the Los Angeles Rams.

When Cowlings's career ended, he became a combination friend, father confessor, and alter-ego to O.J. It was logical, fitting, and perhaps predestined that Cowlings would wind up in the driver's seat of O.J.'s Bronco during the June 17, 1994, non-chase down the San Diego freeway in Los Angeles. (He claimed that he only wanted to protect and calm his friend.) He later spent thirty minutes negotiating with the police for O.J.'s surrender. He was arrested and charged with aiding and abetting the escape of a fugitive, namely O.J.

Immediately after his release from jail, Cowlings refused to talk to reporters. He turned down a million-dollar offer from a tabloid publication for a kiss-and-tell story on O.J. Cowlings did not live his life vicariously or define his identity through a high-profile sports figure. He was his own man.

Jimmy and Eunice Simpson, Cowlings, and many others who remain unnamed, influenced O.J. And they weren't coaches or superstar athletes.

• • • • • •

"*G*od is dead. But O.J. isn't." That was the inscription on the desk of a USC student when O.J. won the Heisman Trophy in 1968. It tells much about the otherworldly intoxication of sports. For many it blurs the line between reality and fantasy. Coaches know this better than anyone. They wheel and deal to ram as many blacks as they can into their school's uniforms. The name of the game is not study, baby, study; but win, baby, win. If coaches in big ticket, high powered and heavily endowed college programs don't win, it's the want ads, baby, the want ads for them. Their job is to win games. Rebounding, scoring and rushing yardage averages are often more important to them than grade point averages. If the players forget that, they'll soon be combing those same want ads.

Major colleges have a huge vested interest in keeping the well-oiled athletic assembly-line moving smoothly. It means hard dollars. In 1989, the NCAA bagged a one billion dollar TV contract for basketball and baseball. Each major NCAA university took in nine million dollars in revenue from its athletics programs. In the two major revenue-generating sports, basketball and football, blacks make up respectively fifty and seventy percent of the college players.

How much exactly is a superstar worth to a college? A lot. Take Georgetown University basketball center, Pat Ewing. Attendance at Georgetown University basketball games jumped more than 100,000 during the four years he played there.

- The revenue increased $4, 426,268.

Pre-Ewing, Georgetown would have been on the tube

maybe six times. With him they were on eighteen times.
- The revenue increase was $1,800,000.

Pre-Ewing Georgetown didn't have a prayer of making it to the NCAA tournament. With Ewing they made it three times, winning the NCAA national championship once.

- The revenue increased $2,250,000.
- During his four years, Georgetown raked in $8,476,268.

Ewing didn't do too badly either. His reward in college was a scholarship worth $48,000 and a degree. He was picked in the first round by the New York Knicks and signed a multi-million dollar contract. Ewing was fortunate. He was a superstar athlete and would make millions in the NBA. He went to a college that believes in graduating its athletes. Many black college athletes aren't as fortunate.

Major colleges tout their athletes as student-athletes. This is a fiction. The paltry stipend the athletes receive for tuition, room, board, and books barely pays their expenses. Many are enticed by wealthy alumni, boosters, and sports agents who often provide them with under-the-table payments, a "no-show" job and illegal contracts. They are victims of a dream.

The aspiring Michael Jordans and Emmit Smiths spend countless hours mastering their dribbling or ball carrying skills with little thought to their future after their sports days are finished. They live for the day when they will sign megabuck pro contracts.

O.J. did. "Money means everything to the ghetto kids who don't have any." Most will never get big paydays playing games as he did. The chance of a black high school athlete making it in the pros is one in 18,000. Only 2.3 percent or 215 of the 9,500 college football seniors will be drafted by the NFL.

Sports sociologist Harry Edwards claims that a high school athlete has more of a chance of getting hit on the head by a meteorite than making a pro team. The talented few that make it don't automatically step off the athletic field and into lucrative business, professional or public careers as do many white athletes or O.J.

The *Washington Post* did a ten-year follow-up on thirty-six basketball players who played for Georgetown and the Universities of Maryland and Virginia in the 1980's. Most told sad tales of failed careers, part-time jobs, unsuccessful tryouts with NBA teams, and barnstorming tours with semi-pro or European teams. Twenty-eight eventually got their degrees and settled into careers as salesmen, teachers, or counselors.

Even though the story is repeated by thousands of other ex-athletes, illusions die hard. A group of black high school athletes were told that the odds against them making a pro team were nearly impossible. Fifty-one percent still believed that they could beat them.

This might all be worth the sacrifice if colleges would educate them. Many still refuse. The 1994 report card on the graduation rates for black athletes at fifty Division I schools was an abomination. The majority of the schools graduated less than one-third of their black players. Four graduated none. The coaches and administrators at these schools go through verbal contortions in an effort to rationalize their failure to educate their athletes. They insist that the non-graduates transfer, drop out of sports or turn pro.

This is nonsense. Only a tiny percent of the more than 8,000 players are eligible for hardship status in the NFL. Few of them choose it. Hundreds of college players will fight for the two or three openings on each NBA team. Most of the athletes don't transfer. Those that drop out succumb to the intense pressure of trying to juggle practice and travel with their supposed classroom duties.

Many athletes waltz through three or four years at colleges and still emerge as educational cripples. Their course curricula is the tip-off. How many algebra, English, history, and chemistry courses do they take? Now, how many physical education, craft, and general studies courses do they take?

Washington Redskins defensive tackle Dexter Manley apparently took a lot. In 1989, he made a teary-eyed confession to the Senate Education Committee that he couldn't read or write. Manley was pursued by many colleges even though he suffered from a childhood learning disorder. He scored six on the college ACT test. The mean score was eighteen.

He wound up at Oklahoma State University where he majored in marketing. He didn't finish. The pro dollars were irresistible and he quickly signed with the Redskins. A career-ending injury to Redskin quarterback Joe Theisman snapped Manley back to the reality that an illiterate black man wouldn't get very far once his glory days in football were over. "It was one play and it was over for him. If that happened to me what did I have?"

The Manley story only became a story when he was arrested for drug possession and was temporarily banned from the NFL. There are almost certainly other athletes in the same boat as Manley who've been shamelessly used by colleges and then dumped after an injury or after their eligibility ran out. The public will never know about them.

O.J. was not an educational cripple like Manley. He had enough sense to make a real effort in the classroom at USC. He told a campus reporter in 1968, "What's the use of going to school if it's just to play football." But he did not graduate. He dropped out the semester before he was scheduled to get a degree in public administration. O.J. was lucky. He had a three-year promotional contract with Chevrolet for $250,000 waiting for him at the end of his senior season. Most college athletes don't.

Manley might have been able to read and write his name, and perhaps O.J. might have graduated, if colleges routinely provided counseling, tutoring, and financial assistance to athletes to encourage them to complete their studies when their eligibility ends.

Some black coaches are troubled that many of their black "student-athletes" end up in dead-end jobs or on the streets hustling or dealing drugs. From 1993 to 1995 they fought the NCAA's attempt to decrease the number of athletic scholarships. They weren't completely successful, but their effort called attention to the fraud of the "student-athlete."

• • • • •

*O.*J. beat the terrible odds and wound up a millionaire, celebrity, and media personality. He got an additional pay-off that most black professional athletes don't. He became a sports icon idolized by millions of whites. There's an age-old cost for that honor.

English philosopher-economist Thomas Carlyle believed that societies exist on hero worship. They create the all-powerful "Great Man." This Olympian-like figure profoundly impacts the public: "Like lightening out of heaven, the rest of men waited for him like fuel, then they would flame." The athletic hero in American life is Carlyle's "Great Man." He is admired and adored.

He is the instant repository of the dreams, delusions, and fantasies of a public desperately in need of vicarious escape. The sports hero seduces, strokes, and comforts the public. He is expected to operate above the fray of human problems and pain. He is expected to raise society's aspirations. Society rewards him for what he is, not who he is.

Football more than any other sport mirrors the best and the worst in American society—competition, greed, selfishness, and violence as well as the spirit of cooperation, organization, achievement, and heroism. It is also an exclusively male preserve, rife with sexism and misogyny. It's perhaps America's main fake masculinity ritual of passage.

Football reinforces the prized male virtues of strength, toughness, and aggression. The male fans that sit in the stands and at home engage in ritual bonding. They identify with players, assume their personality and have a socially-approved outlet to act out aggression, often times against women. The staff at women's shelters routinely puts extra operators on their hot lines during the Super Bowl every year to handle the increased number of complaints of spousal violence.

Football resembles a military camp with a rigid hierarchy, defined roles, iron-clad rules, and an emphasis on discipline and order. O.J. was a prized player. This put him at the top of the hierarchical pecking order and guaranteed him fame, glory, wealth, and fan adulation.

The memory of the sports hero's exploits remains frozen in the public mind even after he slips from public grace. When O.J.'s image changed and he went from hero to accused murderer, his market value soared. Here's a comparison of O.J.'s value pre- and post-arrest:

- 1970 rookie football card: pre-$60, post-$300.
- 1971 football card: pre-$5, post-$75.
- A game jersey: pre-$1500, post-$5,000.
- An O.J. football game board: pre-$20, post-$150.

Signature Rookies Trading Company eagerly insisted that post-arrest O.J. fulfill his contract to sign 1,000 trading cards. No obstacle was too great to get a piece of O.J. A daring thief in broad daylight jimmied a bolt from the floor of one of the trophy rooms at the Pro Football Hall of Fame in Canton, Ohio and made off with a thirty-five pound bronze life-size bust of O.J. A perplexed museum director couldn't figure out why, "It can't be worth anything in the market because you can't sell it." That was an arguable point. But, even if he was right fans and collectors weren't paying and stealing for O.J. They were paying and stealing for a memory of the past.

O.J. did not ask to be anointed a hero. He knew what the cost would be: "You realize if you're living an image, you're just not living."

•  •  •  •  •  •

O.J. had an additional burden. He was a sports icon and he was black. Although he deliberately said little about race, he sensed that much of American society harbors negative images of African-Americans. He knew that there were those who waited for him to slip. During the filming of a television commercial, he slurred a few lines of ghetto slang. He quickly reprimanded himself, "That's what happens when I spend too much time with my boys, I forget how to talk white." O.J. was fortunate. He could "talk white."

O.J. understood what was required of a black icon. He prepped himself for life after football by becoming adroit at playing the commercial game. O.J. along with other black sports icons Michael Jordan and Magic Johnson kept a tight wrap on their political views and personal opinions to maintain their spot on the pedestal.

Jordan was criticized during the Senate election campaign in 1988 for not endorsing liberal Black Democrat Harvey Gant against conservative Republican Jesse Helms in his home state of North Carolina. He had every right to keep quiet. White sports icons Mickey Mantle, Joe Di Maggio, Bob Petit, Bob Cousy and Joe Montana rarely spoke out on political or social issues. They also observed the unwritten rule that sports heroes should be seen and not heard. Even if they occasionally slipped and forgot that rule, the damage was minimal. Society was much quicker to forgive them.

Black superstars don't have that luxury. They are not exempt from racial stereotypes. One misstep can turn the cheers into jeers. The discomfort is immediately seen and felt by the black superstars.

After the *New York Times* in 1993 reported that Jordan was involved in gambling, NBA commissioner David Stern quickly investigated and found that Jordan was not guilty of anything illegal and had committed no rule violations. It did not stop the rumors, innuendoes, and accusations. When Jordan refused to respond to the allegations in the *New York Times,* many sportswriters pounced.

One sports columnist in the *L.A. Times* twisted Jordan's silence to imply that he was guilty of wrongdoing. Another *Times* columnist lectured him on his responsibility to uphold a public image. The pressure of the gambling controversy and the murder of his father probably forced Jordan out of the game for a season and a half when he was at the height of his career.

For a brief time Magic also felt the wrath of some fans and sportswriters when he publicly revealed in November 1991 that he had contracted the HIV virus. He was hounded by rumors, innuendoes, and accusations of sexual profligacy and deviancy. A sports columnist for the *L.A. Times* gave him the same lecture as Jordan, reminding him that he "has a responsibility to be responsible." This certainly played a part in cutting short his NBA playing career. It also cost him major revenue.

Immediately after his announcement, Target, Pepsi-Cola, Nestle's Chocolate, and Kentucky Fried Chicken solemnly swore that he would continue to endorse their products. This was mostly for public consumption. They would have looked like ogres if they had dumped a popular hero who suffered from a tragic illness.

They waited for a few weeks until the furor died down and then quietly dropped him. Johnson lost an estimated twenty-five million dollars in endorsement income. Magic's trademark grin that was so familiar to millions permanently disappeared from the TV sets in America's living rooms.

Magic, Jordan and other athletes have an obligation to exercise decorum in their personal lives. Wild sex and gambling binges aren't virtues. But they should be personally responsible not because society has carved out an artificial fantasy role for them, rather because it's the right thing to do. That goes for anybody.

Even before O.J.'s public tumble there were signs that his marquee value had begun to fade. His contracts worth $400,000 and $550,000 annually with NBC and Hertz would expire in 1995 and 1997. There was no assurance they would have been renewed. If they weren't, he would no longer have been a hot ticket item on the lecture circuit. That would've ended the $10,000 speaking fees that he commanded for motivational talks at corporate gatherings.

During divorce proceedings in 1992, he claimed that his annual income had dropped to about $800,000. This was less than half of what the press reported he earned. A year later, O.J. sold his Laguna Beach townhouse and a condo in Monarch Bay for substantial losses. Following his arrest, a spokesperson for Hertz was candid: "Obviously, Hertz has no plans to utilize Mr. Simpson in future advertising."

There were more indignities. *Time-Life* pulled his picture from the front of its planned book on past Heisman Trophy winners. His nameplate was mysteriously removed from a plaque honoring Heisman Trophy winners at the Downtown Athletic Club in Manhattan.

O.J. suffered the fate of a tarnished celebrity icon toppled from his lofty perch, and the fate of many blacks in the corporate world who were unceremoniously dumped once their usefulness wore out.

• • • • • •

*T*here's a message in the tragic saga of the fallen American sports hero. African-Americans must demand that colleges educate and prepare black athletes for careers outside of sports. But that's not enough. Black professionals and educators must create academic self-help programs to recycle young blacks from sports junkies to serious students. They can provide educational scholarships for academically sound athletes and establish career counseling, job and skills training programs.

Black parents whose sons or daughters are involved in athletic programs must hold coaches, teachers, and school administrators accountable for their children's courses, grades, and campus activities. They must make it clear that if their sons or daughters don't perform in the classroom, they don't get to perform on the field or the court.

Even as O.J. made big plays on the field, there were danger signs. His contract expired in 1973 after his first three years of play with the Buffalo Bills. He had already begun to establish his superstar credentials. O.J. wanted to renegotiate his contract. Bill's owner Ralph Wilson refused. The sportswriters and fans turned vicious. For the first time in his career, O.J. heard the fans boo him when his name was announced. "The cheers weren't there, nor the opportunities. I wondered where everything had gone." The boos eventually turned to cheers when O.J. re-signed. He went on to have several record-breaking years.

That experience was a reminder that sports icons are fragile. Society can break them at any time. The man whose life in some ways paralleled O.J.'s could have told him that. Jackie Robinson knew hardship. His father deserted the family when he was young. In high school and college, he was a phenomenal all-everything athlete. His exploits in baseball, after breaking the color line, are legendary.

In the 1970's, *Sport* magazine voted him the "most significant" athlete of the past quarter-century. When his playing days ended he became a successful and respected businessman and community leader. But Robinson had no illusions about how society saw him. Shortly before his death he reflected, "I was a black man in a white man's world. I never had it made." Neither did O.J.

## eight
# Playing the Race Card

$D$uring a day of golfing at the ritzy Rockland Country Club in New York in 1990, O.J. shrugged off protests over the exclusion of blacks from the Shoal Creek Country Club in Alabama. When one was finally admitted, O.J. was relieved. "All that matters is that they are in, let's get on with it." O.J. was already in one of the exclusive playlands of America's corporate power brokers. The chairman of Hertz sponsored his membership in the super-chic Arcola Country Club in Paramus, New Jersey. At the time of his arrest he was still the club's only black member.

Nonetheless O.J. never denied that racism was still a nasty glitch in American life. He simply felt that it was a transient obstacle that many blacks were overcoming. He believed that his life and career proved that. Prominent professionals, entertainers, athletes, and celebrities like O.J., nurture the illusion among many upwardly-mobile blacks that blacks have nearly attained the American Dream. If so, then the era of political protest is over.

Clarence Thomas is an example. Civil rights leaders, black feminists, and political radicals relentlessly slam him. They call him a traitor, a sell-out and an Uncle Tom. These are the kinder epithets. But a significant number of blacks don't see anything wrong with what Thomas is saying. A *USA Today* poll taken during the 1991 Thomas Supreme Court confirmation hearings debacle reported that many blacks thought that self-help, not quotas and affirmative action should be the goal of blacks.

Not much has changed since then. More than sixty percent of blacks say that they prefer being hired based on test scores rather than "preferential treatment." Many blacks agree with Republican conservatives William Bennett and Dan Quayle that government social programs don't work, welfare dependency must be eliminated, the schools have failed and single parent households are a major problem. More and more blacks denounce big government, support pro-life issues and demand more police, prisons, tougher criminal laws, and the National Guard to crack down on crime.

Many among the black middle-class fervently preach the doctrine of the declining significance of race. It hasn't declined. It has only changed form.

• • • • • •

**S**impson's parents didn't fit into the category of the new upwardly mobile black middle class. Their roots were in the grinding poverty of the farm country of Louisiana and Arkansas. O.J.'s great-grandparents were slaves.

His maternal grandparents raised cotton around their house. When they ran out of money they supplemented their income by sharecropping for white farmers. The young O.J. spent many days during his summertime visits from San Francisco watching his grandparents pick watermelons on a half-acre farm they worked.

O.J.'s father Jimmy had the same Southern dirt farm roots. He chopped cotton for white folks. He joined the army to escape the racism and poverty of rural Arkansas. Following his discharge, he married Eunice and moved to San Francisco. The marriage didn't last. When Jimmy left, Eunice was stuck with four children to provide for. O.J. dreamed of scaling the middle-class ladder of success and escaping the poverty of their Portrero housing project.

As an All-American college and superstar pro football athlete he was on the fast track into the black middle class and beyond. The Portrero housing project days soon became a faint memory. Racism didn't. Attending a wedding with some black friends, he overheard a white woman say, "There's O.J. and some niggers." O.J. didn't shrug that off. "That sort of thing hurts me." For an instant, he realized that blacks could escape the "hood" but America still regarded his acquaintances and, by extension, himself with contempt.

Many of his peers who have moved up the economic ladder are getting mixed racial signals, too. They are legally free to live, sleep, eat, and travel anywhere in America they wish. Their new found prosperity and status, however, does not insulate them from daily insults, slights, and even occasional violence.

In polls taken after the Rodney King beating in 1991, middle-class blacks no matter whether they were politically liberal or conservative were virtually unanimous in their belief that any black person could have been on the ground that night being pulverized by the police.

After the acquittal of the four LAPD officers in 1992, many black professionals blasted the racial double-standard in the criminal justice system. If King was denied justice, they could be denied justice, too.

The King beating and the Simi Valley verdict forced many black professionals, businesspersons, and politicians to take a position that went against their instincts and that would have been unthinkable a year earlier. They refused to condemn the riots. While they would not have personally participated in the rioting, burned property, or beaten whites, they still identified with the rioters.

Anger at the criminal justice system is only the starting point for black middle-class rage. Many of these privileged blacks reject society's attempt to make them visible symbols of progress, while allowing many Americans to think that racism is virtually defunct. They learn to separate surface progress from real progress. They don't delude themselves that they are totally exempt from the rampant racial stereotypes about blacks.

• • • • • •

Question: Do black prosecutors face any special burdens either inside or outside the courtroom?

Answer: On more than one occasion, I've walked into court and the judge has mistaken me for the public defender.

Q: Has the judge ever mistaken you for the defendant?

A: Yes, as a matter of fact, now that you mention it.

When Los Angeles County Deputy District Attorney Christopher A. Darden admitted this to an interviewer he had fifteen years experience as a state prosecutor, was praised by the press, lauded by the legal profession, and patted on the back by much of the public for his performance as a lead prosecutor in the O.J. trial. Yet to many of the men who run the criminal justice system only the thinnest of lines separated Darden from the man he was prosecuting.

Political newcomer J.C. Watts would probably be one of the last to be accused of using racism as a crutch to explain black poverty. He and O.J. were much alike on that point. They had one other thing in common, football. Watts was a state football legend. As quarterback he led the University of Oklahoma to two Orange Bowl victories and a national championship during the 1980's. Whereas O.J. had no known political ambitions nor publicly endorsed or stated a preference for either the Republican or Democratic parties, Watts had solid political connections off the gridiron. He was chairman of the Oklahoma Corporation Commission and a conservative Republican businessman. He was one of twenty-five GOP candidates that ran for Congress in November 1994.

Watts ran in the traditionally conservative Fourth Congressional District. Clinton and the Democrats took only thirty-three percent of the vote in 1992. In 1994, he also had the advantage of riding the crest of voter fury against Democratic incumbents. Watts should have been a shoo-in in a campaign where race shouldn't have counted. His Democratic opponent David Perryman made sure that it did.

Only seven percent of the voters in the district were black. He saturated local TV with pictures of Watts as a twenty-year-old college student sporting an Afro hairstyle and an open neck shirt. There was no overt racial appeal made. Perryman probably hoped that white voters would not see Watts as a conservative Republican businessman but as a black militant. Fortunately for Watts, enough white voters rejected Perryman's not so subtle appeal to race to give him a narrow victory. But race still made the election closer than it should have been.

If anyone could transcend race it was General Colin Powell. His credentials were more impressive than any politician. It seemed that many whites agreed. Sixty-three percent said that he could get enough white support to be elected president in 1996. In a head-to-head race with Clinton, Powell beat him fifty-one to forty-one percent. This was only a straw poll. Powell, of course, hadn't faced the voters.

Powell and O.J. were prominent African-Americans who were practically household names. Throughout their professional careers both refused to use race as a crutch. While O.J. was mostly silent on race, Powell wasn't. He called racism "Exhibit Number one." Ironically and fittingly, his prime exhibit was the vile and racist remarks of former LAPD detective Mark Fuhrman that surfaced in the O.J. trial.

O.J. never had political ambitions, Powell did. If he chose to run for president, he would be grilled hard by the public and the press on foreign and domestic policy issues and even harder on racial issues. Powell would be under an intense looking glass. He wouldn't have much margin for error.

If he stood as a middle-of-the-road moderate and gave all the politically correct answers, there would still be questions. Many would still suspect that an African-American political candidate would automatically show racial favoritism toward blacks. His presidential opponent would look for any sign of reverse-bias.

If a skeleton turned up in Powell's closet, or was placed there, would the press and much of the public presume him innocent and accept his explanations at face value? Or would they rush to condemn him? Would the press and his political opponents use racially-loaded code words to attack him?

*Newsweek* dug a chink into its own political icon. It wondered if the political climate in America was so poisoned and cynical that even he "will prove ephemeral, disposable and unable to carry the burdens imposed by a needy, dissolute nation."

Was this a veiled slap at Powell's personal competency for the job or simply genuine concern that a nation couldn't appreciate a man of his caliber? Why would *Newsweek* ask that about a man who planned military campaigns and advised three presidents? The media never asked that about Ike.

• • • • • •

$O$nce when O.J. was glad-handing a room full of corporate executives, he noticed that other than himself there was
only one other African-American present. He couldn't resist,
and cracked: "Why are we the only two people here." That was
the closest he would come to a complaint that blacks were still
largely outsiders in the business and corporate world and
society. O.J.'s caution was not motivated solely by his desire to
protect his position and status. It was simply his way of trying
to handle a situation he did not create and did not feel he could
change.

In that sense O.J. was no different than many black professionals and businesspersons who find ways to cope with often
daily racial slights and insults. It is a full-time job that many
find distasteful particularly when they are accused of overre-
acting or imagining racial offenses.

This is not generally the case. Most middle-class blacks do
not rush to racial judgment at the first hint of a racial problem.
Most are cautious and evaluate each situation based on past
experiences before deciding whether to take any action. It is
easier for most blacks to endure unpleasant encounters that
may or may not be racially motivated than to expend energy
and time protesting or complaining. But there are many situations in which race is of continuing significance in American
life and that even O.J. could not turn a blind eye to.

*Public places:* Many blacks are subjected to poor (or no)
service, bad seating, long waits, special cover fees, and prepay-

ment requirements in restaurants. The experience is particularly unsettling since it's difficult to determine whether it is deliberate discrimination by management, inattentive waiters, or short-handed help.

Cabs are a constant problem for black business travelers. Many of them stand on curbs, shaking with anger as cabs ignore their signals, then stop a few feet in front of them to pick up whites. Blacks aren't letting their imagination run rampant. A sting by the New York City Taxi and Limousine Commission in 1993 caught 22 of 132 cabbies passing black passengers to pick up whites. Black ex-mayor David Dinkins was one of them. He was refused service in 1994. A Los Angeles cab driver was blunt. "Everybody I know in this business won't pick up black guys."

Cab drivers say they are scared, not bigoted. They have been beaten, robbed, assaulted, and even murdered. Their assailants have been whites, Latinos, Asians, and presumably all of them weren't wearing business suits or designer dresses. Yet they don't refuse to pick them up on sight. What are the odds of a cabby being mugged or murdered by a black businessperson?

In some cities, the unstated rule is that cab drivers won't go into certain areas at any hour. This informal system of redlining penalizes and criminalizes everyone who lives in that section of town.

O.J. received the perks of the corporate world. He was chauffeured from place to place in limousines and company cars. He did not have to risk the indignity of being refused cab service or receiving slow service in a restaurant. But the corporate world has its limits, and it's doors can close even for prominent blacks. When cabs bypassed him, ex-mayor Dinkins discovered that. O.J. might have discovered the same.

*Retail stores and residential neighborhoods:* During the O.J. trial, a prosecution witness who was a neighbor of Nicole's, claimed that he saw a man that resembled O.J. purportedly sitting in a Ford Bronco across from her condo. She lived in a predominantly white middle-class Brentwood neighborhood. The witness became suspicious. He did not know O.J. He did not indicate that the man he claimed might have been O.J. was doing anything suspicious, or looked out of place. The only reason he gave for his suspicion was that the man he thought was O.J. was black.

Blacks are often followed by security guards and ignored by clerks and sales personnel. Many are required to produce ID's or driver's licenses to verify checks and credit cards even when they have accounts. Black contractors, tradespersons, gas, electric, and telephone field service employees are frequently watched, followed and harassed by residents and police when making calls in white (and non-white) neighborhoods. When police and residents are asked why, they simply say that they looked "suspicious."

*Employment:* "I arrived when black became in vogue. All the major companies in the United States were putting out those memorandums." O.J. quickly figured out that during the 1970's the corporate world hungered for talented and educated blacks and would make a special effort to find them. He was one of the first to exploit his sports fame and his color. By the time he left the gridiron he was pitching for RCA, Acme Boots, General Motors, RC Cola, Schick shavers, Foster Grant glasses, Treesweet, Wilson Sporting Goods and, of course, Hertz.

Celebrity Simpson was a shining symbol that blacks had made a permanent and irreversible breakthrough in business and the professions. Meanwhile, many white males were losing ground economically through recession and corporate downsizing. They complained loudly that the employment field had become unleveled against them. They did not express their outrage at the following affirmative action preferences that mostly benefited them:

- GI Bill Benefits
- Special Admissions for Alumni Children
- Agriculture Subsidies
- Senior Citizen Entitlements
- Business Subsidies and Tax Breaks
- Student Athlete Special Placements
- Veterans Credit Toward Civil Service Jobs
- Homeowner Mortgage Tax Write-Offs

Angry white males did express their outrage at affirmative action preferences they imagined only benefited minorities and women, especially court-imposed "quotas." They are, however, rare and have been imposed almost exclusively on a handful of police and fire departments nationally. The *Paradise* decision in 1987 is the only Supreme Court decision that explicitly upheld court-imposed "quotas."

It was widely attacked by conservatives and sparingly read. It required that quotas be tailored to specific jobs in specific agencies. They must be flexible and temporary. There is not one word in the decision that says that whites can't be hired. The court made it clear that hiring has to be "fair" to white applicants and that they could and should be hired if there are no qualified women or minorities.

While many corporations issue press releases, brochures, assorted hand-outs, and annual stockholder reports that boast of their commitment to diversity, a Korn Kerry international survey in 1991 found that less than one percent of the top corporate executives were black. Yet sixty-nine percent of whites in a 1990 National Opinion Research Center poll still believed that a corporation would hire or promote a "less qualified black" before a white.

During the 1990-1991 recession, many corporations hired no blacks and downsized thousands out the door. The share of jobs blacks held at major corporations dropped for the first time in nine years. Hispanics and Asians gained jobs. Black managers made up only 5.2 percent of the total managerial positions for all races.

Whites are also downsized out the corporate door. Many, however, turn around and enter other doors. They are the recipients of what one black manager calls the "FBI syndrome." They have friends, brothers, and in-laws to open new doors for them. Many blacks that lose their jobs do not.

It took sports enshrinement, movie stardom, public relations savvy, and personal charm before O.J. fully attained his fragile insider status in the corporate world. O.J. did not delude himself and think that he could gain that bit of acceptance by becoming a white person. He did something else. He made race a non-issue. O.J. considered this a small price to pay to win respect and avoid being shunned by his corporate peers.

But if O.J. had been treated as a corporate untouchable it would not have been due totally to overt discrimination. There are many state and federal laws that prohibit it. Many would-be black corporate climbers are simply victims of negative racial assumptions. Many managers view them as lazy, incompetent, and less skilled. They are more closely watched and their errors are often magnified. They often receive marginal ratings on their performance evaluations. This adversely affects their chance for promotions.

Black executives report that they are routinely excluded from social functions and discussions of important business decisions. The country clubs where much of America's corporate business is discussed and deal making is done are often closed doors to all but the most affluent and socially-connected blacks. The dress, language, mannerisms, style, and demeanor of even executive position blacks are often considered foreign to many white executives.

Corporate officials are ever alert for any departure from middle-class norms. Most blacks feel intense pressure to conform and are fearful that if they physically associate with other blacks, they will create an instant slum in the office and jeopardize their chance for promotions or other benefits. They go through a ritual that resembles the Japanese custom of distancing, in which a friend or business associate who breeches an unwritten code of conduct is ostracized by peers.

O.J. knew that to play the corporate game he would have to look, act, and talk like a successful executive. He dressed impeccably. He took diction classes. He smiled and joked a lot. He was careful always to be on his best behavior publicly. He was determined not to get caught with his guard down. O.J. did not have the luxury of just being O.J. He had to play a part and live up to the expected image.

• • • • • •

**Business:** O.J. also considered himself a shrewd business-man. For a time, he was. But the business world is fickle and fortunes can turn at any time. O.J. was no exception. Much of the press traced O.J.'s mounting business failures to the de-struction of his Pioneer Chicken franchise during the 1992 L.A. civil disturbances. That was only one factor. The deepening California recession, employee lay-offs, shrinking consumer spending, tighter credit and financing by banks forced him to close three of his eight Honey Baked Ham stores. O.J. was finally confronted with the monumental headaches of the small black business owner.

More than eighty percent of small black businesses fold within two years. This is no accident. The economic infrastruc-ture of the African-American communities is not designed for capital retention or inflow. The iron-clad control of domestic markets by major corporations is akin to a kind of domestic colonialism. Black consumers buy goods from corporate producers and black workers serve as lower paid labor. This near permanent capital flight from black communities virtually ensures that small black businesses are shoved to the outer fringes of the small business economy.

The seemingly unsolvable problem for black business owners is securing capital. In 1992-1993, the *Wall Street Journal* surveyed 500 black entrepreneurs with revenues in excess of $100,000. Ninety percent were turned down by banks for loans. Only six percent of black businesses received any capital from financial institutions. Nearly two-thirds of those paid higher interest rates on their loans than white-owned businesses. While black business has grown steadily in sales and volume of business it still is a poor stepchild in the corporate world.

In 1994, the sales of the top 100 black firms equaled less than the sales of J.P. Morgan Corporation, which ranked number eighty-seven on the 1994 *Fortune 500* list. The total sales of all black businesses in America was a microscopic three percent of the sales of the *Fortune 500* companies.

*Net worth*: There were serious questions about O.J.'s net worth. He told one story—declining fortune(s). Divorce attorneys for Nicole told another—quite wealthy. The media picture of Simpson as a man with a bottomless personal vault was wildly inflated. His corporate income had dropped. He had lost money on his business and property investments. He was still worth a lot, but not what the public and much of the press believed.

The belief that many black professionals with high incomes like O.J. have accumulated vast wealth is an illusion. Nearly thirty percent of black middle-class professionals have incomes that exceed $4,000 gross per month. But they have few tangible assets in stocks, bonds and savings. The average net worth of black workers is twelve times less than that of whites.

*Housing*: When the teen-age O.J. visited his hero Willie Mays's home he was dumbfounded by its splendor. He vowed that someday he would live like Mays. Celebrity O.J. lived better. His 5,752 square foot Tudor estate, enclosed by stone walls and an iron gate, sat on 3/4 acre of land in wealthy Brentwood. His neighbors included celebrity stalwarts Tom Hanks, Michelle Pfeiffer, Meryl Streep, and Roseanne.

O.J. was a topline example of the successful black who supposedly could go anywhere and live anywhere. During the 1980's, about one in three blacks fled to the suburbs. They didn't totally enjoy the hassle free life that O.J. appeared to have lived. Many quickly discovered that the suburbs soon looked like the inner city neighborhoods they thought they had left. In every major metropolitan area, more than seventy percent of blacks were resegregated. More incredibly, in Detroit, Patterson, New Jersey and Gary, Indiana, blacks were more integrated in the central cities than in the suburbs.

A 1990 National Opinion Research Center survey revealed that seventy-five percent of the most educated blacks claimed they had experienced housing discrimination. Affluent black families that lived in predominantly white neighborhoods often experienced insults or social ostracism.

*The image*: The one occasion during the pre-trial skirmishes between the defense and prosecution when O.J. became emotionally involved occurred during the debate over the use of the "N" word. The issue was whether jurors would be offended by the use of the word. Prosecutor Christopher Darden claimed that the word would inflame the jury. Simpson defense attorney Johnnie L. Cochran, Jr. argued that it wouldn't. While Cochran spoke, Simpson wiped his eyes and bent his head forward. Cochran seeing that O.J. was visibly shaken paused and offered him a cup of water.

Cochran and Darden, despite the vitriol of their exchange, agreed on one point—the word, *nigger*, was still widely used in America and symbolized the hatred toward blacks. The "N" word formed a deep invisible bond that united rich and famous blacks like Simpson with the poorest and lowliest of blacks.

O.J. could not be completely oblivious to its meaning and intention. He described incidents where he was driving and some one would call him a *nigger*. For a frozen moment he felt helpless and humiliated. From his jail cell, O.J. decided to publicly confront the issue. In a kind of *mea culpa*, he confessed that he had been wrong to ignore the issue in the vein hope that it would go away. It was sad that it took the ordeal of a double murder charge, jail, a trial, and a possible sentence of life imprisonment for O.J. to admit this. At that late date, he sounded like a desperate man reflexively screaming racism to drum up sympathy among blacks and non-blacks.

Whether O.J. sincerely recognized that racism was still a

powerful force in society and should be fought or was just using the issue to beat a prison sentence, only he really knew. But no matter what his motive it was a welcome admission that he finally understood the bitter truth that many blacks have toiled and sweated for years to get degrees, establish a profession, operate a business and play the mainstream game only to discover that they are still not fully accepted as equals.

• • • • • •

When confronted with racism, prosperous blacks construct defensive shields. They repress anger, minimize slights, ignore insults, and avoid embarrassing situations. Many become strident overachievers to prove their worth, gain public acceptance or neutralize racial hostility. O.J. was the best example.

Yet the moment there's trouble suddenly many blacks, like O.J., remember that racism is still pervasive in American society. Their "blackness" takes on a desperate urgency. During his ill-fated freeway ride in the white Bronco, with the police closing in on him and his world shattered, O.J. placed a call on his cellular phone to his first wife, Marguerite. He pleaded with her to make sure that his "kids have a black influence in their lives."

This is the frustrating class dilemma that faces African-Americans. Middle-class blacks cannot assert themselves or exercise the same power as middle-class white men. Even O.J. couldn't. Jerry Burgdoerfer, Hertz executive vice-president who guided Simpson's corporate career at the company, pointed to his quandary: "He wasn't trying to pass as a white person and he didn't espouse being a black person." O.J. was suspended between two worlds. He belonged to neither.

Many middle-class blacks have imbibed the myth that success depends on brains, talent, hard work, and perhaps a little luck. If they fail or are rejected because of race, they feel hurt and betrayed. Some react to the rejection with anger. Some throw up their defense screens and rationalize. Some write letters, threaten lawsuits, even demonstrate. They may win a promotion, receive a loan, secure a membership in a country club or obtain a business contract. These are small victories that are savored and hopefully encourage others to fight against discrimination. They are also continual reminders that race does matter.

O.J. knew it. He looked at the flagpole at the Rockland Country Club when he began an afternoon of golfing and noticed that an emblem flag had just been raised. He quipped "Must be because there's a black on the course." He was not playing the race card. He meant himself.

## nine
# Justice for Sale

"**I**t's going to be major." O.J. defense attorney Johnnie L. Cochran, Jr. knew the mega-costs of trying a capital case. He was involved in several big money, high profile cases. His clients included Michael Jackson, actor Todd Bridges, and Reginald Denny. O.J. was his biggest case. Cochran estimated that the Simpson defense would cost a minimum of two million dollars. But he wasn't concerned. "We'll spend until the money runs out."

O.J.'s pockets were apparently deep enough for Cochran to say that. In the five years before his arrest, O.J. earned about $1.2 million annually, hawking Hertz cars, and hyping sports events. His net worth was estimated at $10.8 million.

There were two reasons he needed every penny. First, despite his celebrity status, he was an African-American facing a criminal justice system deeply influenced by stereotypes of black men as criminal and sexually menacing. Second, his fate would be decided in a court system where money screams. While O.J.'s possession of money could not entirely cancel out his first handicap, he could buy a measure of justice that most Americans could not.

Americans pay about seventy-five billion dollars yearly to attorneys. In 1989, law firms and legal corporations accounted for about one-fourth of the profits of U.S. corporations. Their revenues far outstripped that of the health care industry which has been under continuous heavy political fire for its astronomic costs.

Simpson paid his attorneys $250 to $650 hourly. He hired a small army of paralegals, private investigators, psychiatrists, and forensic experts. He paid them $75 to $250 hourly. O.J. battled over the DNA tests, and paid $550 for the tests. When the test results were in, he paid DNA experts an estimated $50,000 to explain them in court. He paid the travel costs and expenses for attorneys, their staff, and expert witnesses. He paid for computer research, photocopying, secretaries, clerks, telephone calls, and letters. The total cost for the trial according to conservative estimates was about $50,000 daily, $250,000 weekly and $1 million monthly.

Suppose he wasn't a well-to-do African-American celebrity? How would he have done in a capital case? If he had been tried in Philadelphia, the court would have spent a total average of $605 for investigators, and from $400 to $500 for psychologists for him. That would have purchased an indigent O.J. about an hour or two of time from expert witnesses in court.

Trial expenses drove even a celebrity like O.J. into bankruptcy. His income from endorsements dropped to zero. He was forced to liquidate $1.7 million in the stock and options he held in four companies. This was immediate income. He lost additional millions in future earnings from stocks and income when he was forced to resign from the board of directors of the Forschner Group, the exclusive U.S. and Canadian distributor of the Victorinox original Swiss watch, and the Infinity Broadcasting Company radio broadcast services.

O.J. did not write his blockbuster book *I Want To Tell You* just to tell the world the real story of his life and give his version of the case. He did it for money. The publisher, *Little, Brown*, paid him an estimated $1 to $4 million. The proceeds went entirely for his defense. It was still not enough. Midway through the trial he was forced to tap into a million dollar line of bank credit to pay legal expenses. He put his Rockingham estate up as collateral.

O.J., however, couldn't afford to skimp on his defense. His fate hung squarely on the quality of his attorneys. That's true for any defendant in a capital case. Only an experienced, well-financed defense team can create "reasonable doubt" in the minds of jurors in major capital cases.

Even if their client is convicted, they can present evidence that their client suffered from mental or physical impairment or a history of family abuse. These are the "mitigating factors" jurors must consider to meet the constitutional demand that a sentence is based on "a reasonable and moral response to the defendant's background, character, and crime."

The defendant in a capital case generally will face the best prosecutors in the District Attorney's office who have many years experience in trying capital cases. They stay current on legal changes, precedents, decisions, techniques, and court room strategy. They have unlimited resources, teams of investigators, clerical, and technical staff. They depend on skilled medical, forensic, and mental health experts to present and interpret facts and evidence. They have local police and FBI crime labs at their disposal that utilize state of the art technology to uncover and analyze evidence.

Prosecutors have public consensus about crime on their side. Much of the public equates an individual's arrest with guilt. When a defendant is released because of police error, insufficient evidence, constitutional or procedural violations, many politicians and much of the public howl that weak laws and bleeding-heart judges permit criminals to escape punishment. Some state and local court judges who have tried to uphold the law fairly and impartially have been defeated at the polls or have been the targets of successful recall campaigns.

Prosecutors also have the jury system. The mostly middle-class white men and women to whom prosecutors present their evidence to usually reflect middle-class attitudes. Many are also swayed by the thirteenth juror—racism.

• • • • • •

*L*os Angeles County District Attorney Gil Garcetti was disturbed when "jurors" in several mock trials found O.J. "not guilty." He was probably more disturbed when a spokesperson in his office said that prosecutors found that the people they spoke to were reluctant to convict him. But Simpson's attorneys knew that fake jurors in mock trials wouldn't decide his fate. A real jury would.

He had as much reason to worry as the prosecutors. But O.J. had spent much of his professional life wrapped in the tight cocoon of societal hero-worship and adulation. He had faith that the American justice system was fair. He believed that there was someone among the twelve jurors who would decide his fate, who loved and admired "the Juice" and wouldn't believe he could commit such a heinous crime. It was all a bad nightmare that would end once he told them his story.

He was so convinced that the jurors would believe his story and find him not guilty that he became edgy, nervous, and depressed while waiting for the trial to begin. He had pleasant visions of going trick-or-treating with his kids on Halloween, of having Thanksgiving dinner with them, and spending Christmas with his family.

The misery of his plight propelled him to his feet during the early stage of jury selection. He shouted, "I'm an innocent man. I want to get to the jury. I want to get to a jury. I want to get it over with as soon as I can." O.J. really believed that the trial was a mere formality and that an acquittal was a foregone conclusion.

His attorneys knew that prophesying how jurors would vote in major trials was risky business. If O.J. had paid closer attention to recent events in Los Angeles he would have known that, too. The four LAPD officers accused of beating Rodney King were acquitted by a Simi Valley jury in 1992 when much of the world expected a conviction.

The four young men accused of beating Reginald Denny were convicted on lesser charges in 1993 when much of the public thought they would be convicted on all charges. The jurors deadlocked in the 1994 trial of the Menendez brothers who admitted murdering their parents, when much of the public thought that they would be convicted.

O.J.'s attorneys weren't gambling on public sympathy to free him. The defense selected a crack jury selection firm, Trial Logistics. They were one of the leaders among private firms that help defense attorneys pick pro-defense jurors. The firm helped attorneys with juror selection in the McMartin Preschool and the Night Stalker cases, as well as the trial of the four LAPD officers accused of beating King.

They were one of 350 firms that had sprouted up and turned jury selection into one of the legal profession's fastest growing, go-go industries. The firms applied mass marketing techniques such as polling, focus groups, and demographic studies to pick the "right" jury. If prosecutors hired them, the firms tailored their techniques to get jurors likely to convict.

O.J. paid Trial Logistics to devise a questionnaire to weed out jurors who might be biased against him. The core questions were geared to measure prospective jurors' attitudes on race, interracial marriage, and sexual relations. These were all emotional and highly charged issues that unleashed deep personal passions and prejudices.

It would require delicate skill in framing the questions to get truthful answers from juror prospects. Questions on interracial marriage, for example, might read this way: "How

would you feel if your child were in an interracial marriage?"
"Do you have objections to interracial couples having a child?"
"Do you think interracial marriages have a chance to suc-
ceed?" The trick was to find jurors who could put aside those
passions and prejudices and be objective.

• • • • • •

*T*he Sixth Amendment requires that a defendant receive a
fair trial by "an impartial jury." But justice can be neither fair
nor impartial when race lurks in the shadow of the jury box.
Most jurisdictions still pick jurors from voter registration and
tax assessment lists. Black defendants are still tried by mostly
older, white middle-class jurors. The U.S. Supreme Court
explicitly forbids prosecutors from using peremptory challenges to exclude blacks from juries. They don't have to.

Prosecutors and defense attorneys have the same number
of challenges. In most court jurisdictions there are far fewer
blacks than whites in the jury pools. In Los Angeles County in
1994, whites made up fifty-eight percent of those eligible to
serve; blacks made up only fourteen percent.

Defense attorneys run out of prospective black jurors faster
than prosecutors run out of whites. The whites are much more
likely to reflect conservative, middle-class values and beliefs.
Prosecutors want them on juries for another reason. They're
more likely to believe them. The prosecutor's opinion carries
the official stamp of the government. Conservative whites are
more likely to believe the testimony of police and prosecution

witnesses than black defense witnesses and defendants.

Many think that blacks are more likely to lie than whites. The constant media and Hollywood typecasting of young black males as crime-prone, drug dealing "gangstas" has made many whites (and some blacks) more fearful of them. When a group of whites were shown a picture of a black man shoving a white man, seventy-five percent labeled his action "violent behavior." They were then shown a picture of a white man shoving a black man with the same force. Only seventeen percent labeled his action "violent behavior."

Racial typecasting only partly explains the hugely varied response to the same act. The other explanation is ignorance. Black lifestyles, language, body cues, and mannerisms are often uncharted territory to many middle-class whites. They misunderstand, misread, or are hostile to any type of behavior that departs from middle-class norms. Black defendants consequently do poorly. Juries convict them faster, recommend longer prison sentences, and require them to serve longer terms before being eligible for parole.

The same adherence to middle-class norms holds true for many black jurors. Much of the media, the public, and some prosecutors still believe the fiction that black jurors are inherently more sympathetic to black defendants. The media exaggerated the racial conflict between black and white jurors in the Denny beating trial and the federal civil and criminal trials of the LAPD officers convicted of beating King. They cited statements in which some black jurors expressed their opinion that the officers in the King cases got off too lightly, and that they were unwilling to convict the young men that beat Denny of the more serious charges. Those were the exceptions.

Simpson was tried in the Central District Court of Los Angeles County which has the highest percentage of jury eligible blacks in Los Angeles County. It appeared that the prosecution and defense attorneys were intent at the start of jury selection on skirmishing and jockeying to get as few or as many black jurors as possible impaneled. This fed public suspicions that black jurors would allow him to stroll out of court a free man.

• • • • • •

Some blacks were also suspicious of the prosecution. They charged that the prosecutors were trying to eliminate all blacks from the jury panel. There were a few questions on the 294 question sheet the prosecutors used to question prospects that appeared aimed exclusively at blacks. The questions asked applicants to indicate their reading choices among ten newspapers.

One of them was the local black newspaper, the *Los Angeles Sentinel*. *The Korea Times*, *La Opinion* and *Rafu Shimpu* were not listed. The blacks suspected that the prosecution was trying to slip racism into the jury selection process through the back door.

During the early stage of jury selection, the defense continuously tried to score racial points on the jury issue. They accused the prosecution of "badgering" a black juror and charged that the prosecutors were questioning prospective blacks longer and more aggressively than whites, Asians or Latinos. They insisted that this was a deliberate attempt by the prosecution to remove blacks from the panel.

It wasn't. The prosecutors were mindful of the California Supreme Court ruling in 1978 that strictly forbade prosecutors from using peremptory challenges to exclude jurors based on race or religion. If there was any hint that they were discriminating, defense attorneys could demand an immediate judicial review.

Many legal and media commentators, hostile to Simpson, were strangely allied with the blacks who charged that the prosecution was "targeting" black jurors for removal. They bought their own spin that blacks were hopelessly blinded by racial allegiance to a "brother." Seventy percent of the attorneys polled immediately after jury selection was completed predicted that the jurors would deadlock or vote to acquit Simpson. The press repeatedly pounded it home that Simpson would probably walk.

Contrary to their belief, blacks do not think and speak with one racial mind. Michael Knox, a dismissed juror and black, should have put that ridiculous notion to rest for good when moments after he left the courthouse he told the press that the prosecution was presenting an effective case. He later hinted that he "was leaning toward a guilty verdict." Knox cashed his convictions into a quickie kiss-and-tell book he hoped would hit the bestseller charts. Knox may have been driven by fantasies of instant fame and fortune (the book was written by a columnist for the *National Enquirer* if that gives a clue), but he was probably telling the truth about how he felt toward the prosecution.

If the Simpson trial watchers had been alert, they would have figured out that gender, income level, education, and life experiences are variables that are just as important as race in determining how a juror will decide a case. When jurors of diverse ethnic groups deliberate together they are capable, momentarily at least, of putting aside their individual biases.

Even dismissed Simpson juror Jeanette Harris's dynamite revelations to the press that three white Los Angeles County Sheriff's deputies assigned to guard the jurors harassed and intimidated black jurors, and gave preferential treatment to white jurors, did not change this. After Judge Lance Ito ordered the deputies reassigned, four black women jurors disputed nearly everything that Harris said about the deputies.

Juror 98 said that the deputies expressed sympathy when her sister died. Another juror said that they were "professional and kind." Another juror bluntly said that "they got a raw deal." It didn't stop there. Juror 72 criticized a 72-year-old black male alternate juror for complaining about racism, "I don't look at what happened when I was a kid coming up." Only the most die-hard of believers in the all-blacks-think-alike illusion could continue to ignore the difference in black opinions.

In any case, the black Simpson jurors quickly made those who repeatedly promised everyone that blacks could not be objective look silly. They joined with white and Latino jurors to briefly "boycott" the trial in protest over the treatment of the deputies and to call attention to their own personal gripes.

In one action he took, Ito did nothing to put the issue of race to rest. He bounced black postal service supervisor Willie Cravin from the jury. This triggered suspicions that he conspired with prosecutors to racially target jurors. The official reason was that Cravin "intimidated" a non-black female juror. Ito later cited six more incidents of juror intimidation supposedly committed by the 200 pound Cravin. Ito offered no independent corroboration of these incidents, at least publicly.

While some jurors may have perceived Cravin's mannerisms as offensive, almost certainly he was removed as a political concession to the prosecutors. They were furious that Ito had earlier in the day dumped the "intimidated" non-black juror and the day before a white female juror. Prosecutors considered both sympathetic to them. Clark bluntly told Ito that Cravin was "a very severe and grave danger to the integrity of the jury and to their ability to evaluate the evidence." That was her conclusion and hers alone. It was a claim that was impossible to substantiate, particularly since the evidence had yet to be presented to the jury.

The press, nonetheless, predictably labeled Cravin "pro-defense." There was not a shred of evidence that Cravin leaned toward the defense. He had made no statements, pro or con, about Simpson before or during the trial. He had not exhibited any body language, facial expressions, or physical signs that indicated he disapproved of the evidence presented by the prosecutors against Simpson during the six months that he sat on the jury. Few media or legal commentators bothered to second-guess Ito on this point.

A judge in theory can only excuse a juror before jury deliberation if there is tangible evidence that the juror is biased or partial toward the defense or prosecution. Did Ito have that evidence against Harris and Cravin? "He didn't tell me who my accusers were," said an angry Cravin, "he didn't give me a chance to face them." Neither Cravin, Harris, the defense, the prosecution, the media nor the public could really know the truth since Ito made the decision to remove them (and other jurors) in private and promptly sealed the transcripts.

Eventually, Ito, after a legal challenge by the ACLU and news organizations, parceled out sanitized versions of the transcripts to the press. This was little consolation to the dismissed jurors. Much of the public probably still believed that they, rather then the defense or the prosecution, had been guilty of bad judgment, misconduct, or had violated some unstated judicial rule.

Ito appeared to violate the long established legal precept that transcripts of juror misconduct are considered matters of public record and must not be sealed. This is done so as not to fan public and media suspicions that trial proceedings are rigged or manipulated, and the legal system is unfair. These, of course, were the very things that much of the public already believed about the Simpson trial.

It didn't help allay suspicions that Ito and the prosecutors had colluded to knock-off certain jurors, specifically Cravin, when Marcia Clark danced a jig in the courthouse hallway after Cravin got the boot and Christopher Darden quipped to Johnnie Cochran that "we got one of your boys." Darden and Clark swore straight-facedly to the press that no one should attach any special significance to their clownish display of euphoria over Cravin's removal. But many did.

For his part, Cravin said that he had doubts about some of the evidence against Simpson. But he took great pains to assure that he had not formed an opinion about Simpson's guilt or innocence. The outspoken Harris was roundly attacked by many legal experts and media commentators when she complained about the treatment of the jurors and indicated she was less than impressed by the prosecutors. She was accused of practically voting to acquit Simpson before the trial had barely begun.

Harris saw it differently: "It doesn't mean I see Mr. Simpson as innocent. I presume he's innocent. And there's a big difference." Harris understood the Constitution better than some of her critics. Presumption of innocence is the cornerstone of the law. If it wasn't, then why even bother to have trials in the first place? In any case, it was too little too late for both of them.

• • • • • •

*P*rosecutors in Los Angeles and other big cities have tried enough criminal cases to know that black jurors aren't instinctively predisposed to acquit black defendants. In trials in the downtown Los Angeles court, particularly murder trials, black jurors have frequently voted to convict blacks. The proof was as near as three courtrooms down from the Simpson trial. While the prosecution presented its case against him, a jury with two blacks convicted of murder and voted the death penalty for Ernest Dwayne Jones, a black man and former football player.

Both Simpson prosecution and defense critics also ignored something else. Blacks are more likely to be victims of crime, or to have friends or relatives who have been crime victims than whites. They have a greater vested interest than whites in putting violent criminals away. This outweighs any racial loyalties.

Much of the press after the King beating played up the police/black conflict. This presented the distorted picture that the police and black communities are perpetually at war. This is mostly myth. Immediately following the Los Angeles civil disturbances nearly as many blacks as whites said that the police were doing a good job in battling crime. With crime a threat, who else would blacks turn to for protection other than the police? They pay their taxes too and have a right to expect that protection.

Blacks are also aware that once in the jury box they are under greater public scrutiny to make sure that they don't "lean" toward black defendants. They listened intently, and often put more emphasis on the evidence presented by prosecutors, and the testimony of victims and police than the defendants. Reporters and courtwatchers generally agreed that the black jurors took copious notes when the prosecution presented its physical evidence and closely followed the testimony of police and expert witnesses. They showed no signs of disinterest or hostility toward the prosecutors.

If the prosecutors in the Simpson case hadn't believed that black jurors could be fair they would have used each of their twenty peremptory challenges to get rid of as many blacks as they could. They used only ten. The prosecutors followed the law to the letter because they knew that the odds were still with them.

Prosecution critics and defense attorneys were wrong. The object of the Simpson prosecutors was never to eliminate *all* blacks from the jury. From the start of jury selection, Garcetti was resigned that the jury would be predominantly black. He swore that he was not concerned with race but that the jurors "follow their oath to base his or her decision strictly on the law, and the evidence." There was little doubt that when Garcetti and the prosecutors saw an opportunity to massage, influence and, perhaps, subtly tinker with the jury to tilt it in their favor, they would take it. But Garcetti's objective was never to eliminate *all* blacks from the jury, only to get the blacks that they considered the right kind of jurors.

They knew that while the defense banked on a hung jury and mistrial, the odds were less than one in ten they would get it. They also knew that the expected juror dismissals, defections, and "targeting" of black jurors for elimination as the defense charged, wouldn't significantly alter the jury's racial make-up. Most of the alternates also were black.

• • • • • •

*P*rosecutors also employ other tactics to make jury selection appear racially neutral in high stakes trials. Jury sequestering is one. They argue that sequestering is necessary to shield jurors from adverse trial publicity. Garcetti requested this in the Simpson trial. The defense attorneys opposed sequestering. Full sequestering requires the jurors to live in a hotel during the trial. The tactic, if successful, decisively shifts the class and racial deck in the prosecutor's favor.

In a long trial generally older, wealthier persons have the time and resources to spend months on a jury. People of color, women, and younger persons don't. When told that the trial could last up to six months, and that they might be sequestered, more than half of the 900 potential jurors called and immediately asked to be released. Unfortunately for the defense, before the start of the trial the prosecution barraged the media with a long list of alleged acts of domestic violence by Simpson. The defense reluctantly agreed that the jury should be sequestered. They were.

The bigger problem for the defense was not the prosecution's legal methods but juror dishonesty. Many potential jurors withheld information or lied. Researchers observed thirty-one criminal trials. Afterwards they interviewed 190 jurors. They found that twenty-five percent of them falsely denied that they or a family member had been a crime victim. Thirty percent did not reveal that they knew a law enforcement officer.

Many whites are willing to openly express their distrust or hostility toward blacks on radio talk shows or with friends. But few want to be exposed as racial bigots under formal questioning by defense attorneys or prosecutors in open court.

The prosecution also worried that juror dishonesty might cut the other way and that some of the prospective jurors might try to conceal their sympathies to Simpson, or to get their fifteen minutes of fame might lie to get on the jury. One Simpson prosecutor quipped that the jurors should be given lie detector tests. She was only being half-facetious.

If some jurors are impaneled whom they perceive "tilt" toward a defendant in a capital case, prosecutors have other weapons in their legal arsenal to counter. In nearly every jurisdiction in the country, prosecutors exploit the hidden racial and personal biases of jurors and get away with it. There have been documented cases during the 1980's and 1990's where prosecutors called black defendants "nigger," "black gorilla," "bastards," and "superfly," when the alleged victim(s) were white. Some used mock "ghetto" slang to demean black defense witnesses. Some of the cases have been overturned on appeal. Most haven't.

When there are blacks (no matter how few) and whites on a jury, courts almost never overturn a conviction of a black defendant:

- If the prosecution witnesses and the defendant are of the same race;
- If the defendant and the victim are of the same race;
- If the prosecutor makes a post-objection apology to the jury for making a racial reference;
- If a prosecutor refers to the defendant's race for "identification" purposes;
- If a prosecutor claims that race was mentioned for

"merely descriptive reasons;"

- If a prosecutor claims that a racial reference was made in order to question factual statements, or to refute the defense attorney's arguments;
- If the racial reference is impersonal, such as "those people," or "They're not like us."

Courts are loath to reverse a conviction partly because of time and cost and partly because of race. They refuse to believe that whites can't be race-neutral when they judge blacks. Many of the men and women in black robes who sit on the bench are trapped by their own myths about race. They think that racism comes with white sheets and crosses, and *nigger*-baiting demagogues. Few Americans are violent racists of the Klan or Aryan nation type anymore.

The result is that many whites can't or are unable to distinguish between overt racism and the subtle racism embodied in social distancing and the use of code words. O.J., after his sudden conversion to racial critic, didn't make the distinction between the various shades of racial expression either. He concluded that racism "is everywhere I look." But whites aren't by definition racial bigots. Whites that display personal racism more likely have merely incorporated many of the same negative beliefs and perceptions about blacks. If defense attorneys could make a *prima facie* case that a prosecutor played the race card with jurors to get a conviction, a higher court would still require them to prove it was done intentionally. This would be virtually impossible to do even for Simpson's "dream team" attorneys.

Defense attorneys would have to get inside the heads of prosecutors. If psychologists routinely dispute each other's interpretations of individual human motives, what chance would most defense attorneys have of pinpointing hidden prosecutorial racial bias? Most don't even bother to try. For the few that do, the courts usually dismiss their appeals on the grounds that the prosecutor committed "harmless errors" that didn't affect the outcome of the case. The Supreme Court regards racial "slips" by prosecutors as no harm no foul.

The only exception is in a capital case when a black is sentenced by an all-white jury. This was not the case with Simpson. The prosecution was too smart for that. They made no overt racial appeals to jurors. And O.J. was a celebrity, not a poor black defendant. But he knew that in a trial anything could happen if the thirteenth juror—racism—is allowed to cast the deciding vote. It does against many poor blacks and Latinos.

• • • • • •

*M*any of them sit on death rows or receive long prison sentences. When they were convicted, juries often did not consider any "mitigating circumstances." Their court-appointed attorneys could not, would not or didn't know how to present any of those circumstances to a court. Celebrity O.J. by his own admission ignored the occasional news stories about poor defendants denied justice.

O.J. wasn't merely callous or indifferent toward them. At

one time he was poor and probably knew that there were thousands of people who might not have been jailed or convicted if they could have afforded proper legal counsel. O.J. 's wealth removed him from their world and induced personal amnesia to his past. Now that he was a defendant it was a different story. He realized that without money "I would have no chance."

Former Supreme Court Justice Thurgood Marshall did not share celebrity O.J.'s disinterest or naiveté. He was shocked to discover that federal reports bulged with pitiful examples of their shoddy legal representation. There was good reason. *The National Law Journal* checked the professional records of 1,000 attorneys that handled nearly 100 death penalty cases in six states between 1976 and 1991. They found the attorneys who handled capital cases were three to forty-six times more likely to have been disbarred, suspended or disciplined than attorneys who didn't. In interviews with sixty lawyers whose clients are on death row, half said it was their first case.

While states wouldn't dare think of not setting competency standards for accountants, nurses, plumbers, and contractors before issuing them licenses, state courts regularly allowed practically anyone with a law degree to represent defendants in capital cases.

A disgusted Marshall fumed, "capital defendants frequently suffer the consequences of having trial counsel who are ill equipped to handle capital cases." There are 20,000 homicides in America yearly. Yet only 250 or so men receive the death penalty. Many were unlucky enough to be represented by one of those "ill equipped" attorneys.

They weren't alone. In 1992, eighty percent of felony defendants were represented by grossly overworked, underpaid public defenders or court appointed attorneys. Only eleven of the thirty-six death penalty states had public defender offices. Less than half of them had funds to hire investigators, clerks, or secretaries.

Only five percent of indigent defendants saw an attorney before their first court appearance. A harried public defender in Atlanta bluntly described how he dealt with seventeen indigent defendants: "I met 'em, pled 'em and closed 'em—all in the same day." If they were black and accused of crimes against whites, the chances are they received harsher sentences.

The Supreme Court has done little to insure that poor blacks or Latinos get the kind of quality defense that O.J. bought. The Court has mocked the Sixth Amendment. It refuses to require states to spend money to provide competent, trained counsel and staff for poor defendants. In some states, paralegals and law clerks who work on civil rights and civil litigation cases are paid more than attorneys who represent indigents in capital cases.

Texas, which has executed more prisoners than any other state, pays defense attorneys $800 maximum for a capital case. This is not the complete picture. Not one penny comes from the state treasury; the counties must pay for all indigent defense.

The maximum amount other states allocate for capital cases is only marginally better: Alabama, $1,000; Kentucky,

$2,500; and New Mexico, $4,000. Virginia is the stingiest: defense attorneys receive $350.00 maximum for felony cases. Ohio is at the top of the scale. It pays defense attorneys the princely sum of $6,000.

The Oregon Criminal Defense Lawyers Association revealed that an attorney doing exclusively indigent defense work would earn an incredible $72.00 yearly. In many jurisdictions the maximum fees the courts pay attorneys don't cover their hourly overhead costs.

Some counties cut even more corners on indigent defense by borrowing a technique from the construction industry. They put out a contract and often accept the lowest attorney bid. Since attorneys are still free to continue to solicit business from paying clients while they represent an indigent defendant, it's not hard to figure out which client will receive the most time and attention. Many attorneys reason that the county paid for a "no-frills" defense and that's exactly what a poor defendant should get.

• • • • • •

*T*he Simpson case blinded the public to the gaping disparity in the treatment of rich and poor defendants. It fueled the public fear that attorneys are mangling the system and their guilty clients are walking away scot free. Media commentators and legal experts branded the legal system corrupt and compromised and demanded more power and resources for judges and prosecutors, shorter trials, non-unanimous jury verdicts (to convict), and even that the adversarial system be scrapped. This made for good copy and soundbites, but it was absurd.

The Simpson case was an aberration and an illusion from the start. The court installed a $200,000 computer system for the trial. Prosecutors and defense attorneys used the system to present evidence to the jurors on an overhead big screen. The attorneys viewed the evidence on fifteen inch monitors.

Computerized viewing systems are used sparingly in major civil trials and almost never in criminal trials. But then less than one in ten criminal cases ever get to trial anyway. They are plea bargained. In the cases that are tried, the judges and prosecutors have the overwhelming resources and legal means to control, shape, and influence a case. Court-appointed attorneys and public defenders do not. Trials do not drag on for weeks or months but end quickly. In the majority of cases, the defendants are convicted. Few individuals with wealth and influence wind up in the criminal justice system to begin with. Those that do routinely use their money to often successfully evade severe punishment.

Poor criminal defendants that are guilty, and even some that are innocent, generally suffer the full wrath of the system. Since the Supreme Court ruled that defendants have no right to a court-appointed counsel to review or appeal their convictions, many of them spend long years in prison or on death row. If Simpson had not been a wealthy superstar celebrity and ex-football great, he might well have been doomed from the start to have been one of them.

The poor are trapped between the public's desperate fear

of crime and the crass and often bigoted manipulations of those fears by politicians. They can't turn to the courts for help. The courts refuse to: set minimum standards of training and experience for defense attorneys who work on capital cases; encourage jurisdictions to pull names of prospective jurors from welfare rolls, telephone directories, utility customer lists, renter lists or Department of Motor Vehicle lists to get a more ethnically representative juries; and minimize the power of trial consultants to stage manage and manipulate juries.

These defendants can't turn to legislatures for help either. Few legislators have the political courage to defy the media and public opinion and raise the sub-minimum wage that defense attorneys get for defending the poor. This ensures that attorneys will make even fewer challenges to the discriminatory application of the death penalty.

O.J. didn't have to worry about any of these things. He knew that if he was convicted, he would appeal. It would cost plenty. But if his pockets were still deep enough, he had another chance to buy justice.

## Conclusion
# Race, Sex, and Class Lessons for America

*I*n late September 1994 hundreds of persons filed into the downtown court in Los Angeles. They were summoned as prospective jurors in the O.J. Simpson trial. An army of reporters from all over the world was also in and around the court. The TV networks had set up a communications satellite city across from the building that resembled a lunar space exploration station. Much of the public remained fixated on the case.

A few miles away James Foster sat in a Santa Monica courtroom. One reporter from a local newspaper, a TV reporter, and a handful of spectators watched. Foster was on trial for killing his wife Maria. There were remarkable similarities to the O.J. case. Foster was black. He was nearly the same age as O.J. He had two young children. There were allegations that he had abused his wife. He was accused of stabbing her repeatedly. Foster had fled to avoid arrest. Maria, like Nicole, was white.

There were obvious differences. O.J. was a superstar athlete, a celebrity, and media personality. Millions considered him an all-American hero. He was represented by an expensive high-powered "dream" legal defense team. Foster was not wealthy. He was defended by a court-appointed attorney. The evidence was fairly convincing that Foster had committed the murder.

O.J. pleaded innocent and battled for months to try to win acquittal. O.J. was wealthy, prominent and could afford to buy justice. Foster couldn't. O.J. won the sympathy and goodwill of millions. Foster couldn't. O.J. was a *cause celebre* in the media. Foster was ignored and forgotten.

But there were points where the distance between the two men closed. O.J.'s wealth and prominence did not completely shield him from the centuries of sexual and racial myths. O.J. had a white wife. For three centuries interracial sex and marriage were crimes in America. This ignited passions and mob violence. In 1967, the Supreme Court removed the legal stigma from interracial marriage. Society tried to remove the social stigma. It failed. Many whites and blacks still frown on interracial marriage or relationships. It is still America's last taboo.

O.J. was accused of battering his wife. The issue of domestic violence zoomed into public debate. For decades the courts, legislatures, and public agencies had ignored it. When America finally acknowledged it, prominent African-Americans such as Clarence Thomas, Mike Tyson, and Michael Jackson suddenly became the poster boys for sexual misconduct. This reinforced racial and sexual stereotypes, and transformed the issue of male menace into black male menace.

The explosion of black violence, the glorification of the "gangsta" image in film and song and the enshrining of black male toughness painted a grim picture of black self-destruction. Many non-blacks (and some blacks) were convinced that young black males were a threat to society. As always, they were mostly a threat to themselves.

O.J. made good copy. Much of the mainstream media traded responsible journalism for tabloid sleaze. It filled news pages and TV programs with rumors, half-truths, and lies to titillate and tantalize the public.

O.J. exposed the deep racial and class double-standard in the criminal justice system. The District Attorney presumed him guilty almost before his arrest and confidently talked of certain conviction after his arrest. This was a grim reminder that much of America had made crime and punishment a racial problem, not an American problem. But O.J. also had wealth and fame. He was able to buy a measure of justice routinely denied the poor.

O.J. made much of America race-weary. Angry, and sometimes violent, white males were frustrated that they had lost economic ground. They blamed their losses on affirmative action, civil rights, and tax-and-spend Democrats.

They denied that racism and poverty were continuing problems. They launched a ruthless search for enemies and found them among blacks, the poor, welfare recipients, immigrants, and women. They revived and embraced wacky theories that blacks are genetically inferior. The Republicans caught the mood, recycled the old code words—"less government," "welfare cheats," and "crime in the streets,"—and won a smashing electoral victory. They promised to roll back the social clock with their "Contract with America."

The revolt of angry white males heightened black fears and paranoia. Many blacks remembered the near-century of government repression of black leaders from Marcus Garvey to Martin Luther King, and organizations from the NAACP to the Black Panthers.

But they forgot that many whites had a proud and honorable track record of support for civil rights and black progress. Many whites did not instantly presume that O.J. was guilty, even though the victims were white. Many blacks circled the wagons, spun theories of genocidal plots and conspiracies, and rushed to defend a wealthy black man who spent most of his professional career publicly avoiding racial issues.

O.J. symbolized the progress and the failure of the black middle-class. More of them were educated, had better jobs, owned businesses, and had attained middle-class comforts. But many prominent blacks also discovered that society still viewed them as social pariahs. The acquittal in a Simi Valley court of the four LAPD officers who beat Rodney King by a jury with no blacks was a jolt to many middle-class blacks. They found that race still mattered in America.

O.J. was a beloved sports icon. He forgot that celebrity heroes are shallow projections of society's fantasies, delusions, and insecurities. He forgot that icons are fragile. When they tumble they break.

O.J. stood at the center. He played the corporate game. He lived a princely lifestyle. He had what appeared to be a charmed marriage. He was a man who symbolized everything but stood for nothing. He was proof that many Americans had forgotten how to talk to each other about race, sex, and class. He was a warning that it was time for them to remember.

# References

### *Introduction* • Beyond *O.J.*

P.2.    *Wall Street Journal*, March 22, 1995, 1.
P.3.    *Life Magazine*, April, 1995, 18.

### *one* • The Last Taboo: Interracial Marriage

P.5.    Richard Wright, *Native Son*, (New York: Harper & Row, 1966) 307.
P.6.    "The Double Life of O.J. Simpson," *Newsweek*, August 22, 1994, 42.
P.7.    O.J. Simpson, *I Want To Tell You*, (Boston: Little, Brown & Co., 1995) 74.
P.7.    Michael Ortiz Hall, "Dreaming in Black and White," Los Angeles *Times Magazine*, December 11, 1994, 26.
P.8.    Coramae Richey Mann, *Unequal Justice: A Question of Color* (Bloomington, Ind.: Indiana University Press, 1993) 122-123.
P.9.    Al-Tony Gilmore, *Bad Nigger! The National Impact of Jack Johnson* (Port Washington, NY: Kennikat Press, 1975) 95, 100.
P.10.   Randy Roberts, *Papa Jack* (New York: Free Press, 1983) 66-67, 144-146.

P.11.   Roi Ottley and William J. Weatherby, *The Negro in New York*, 1626-1940 (New York: Praeger, 1967) 153-154.

P.11.   *Dallas Herald*, August 19, 1990, 10.

P.12.   For a revealing analysis of sentencing disparities between black and whites within the American criminal justice sytem see Ronald Barri Flowers, *Minorities and Criminality* (New York: Greenwood Press, 1990); and, Marjorie Zatz, Racial, Ethnic Bias in Sentencing, #1 *Journal of Research in Crime and Delinquency*, (1987) 69-92.

P.12.   *LAT*, Oct. 30, 1994, 1.

P.13.   Simpson, *I Want To Tell You*, 81.

P.13.   *New York Times*, December 29, 1991, 4.

P.14.   Simpson, *I Want To Tell You*, 122.

P.14.   Mark Mathabane and Gail Mathabane, *Black and White: The Triumph of Love over Prejudice and Taboo* (New York: Harper & Collins, 1992) 21-44.

P.14.   Andrew Billingsley, *Climbing Jacob's Ladder: The Enduring Legacy of African-American Families* (New York: Simon and Schuster, 1992) 247.

P.15.   *Washington Post*, June 24, 1994, D1.

P.15.   *Wave Newspaper*, July 13, 1994, 4.

P.16.   *Jet*, July 18, 1994, 3.

P.16.   *Sports Illustrated*, June 27, 1994, 21.

P.16.   *NYT*, December 2, 1991, 4.

P.16.   *Ebony*, September, 1994, 42.

P.16.   Mathabane, *Black and White*, 200.

P.17.   Abbey Lincoln, "Who Will Revere The Black Woman" in Toni Cade, *The Black Woman* (New York: Penguin, 1970) 83.

P.17.   Eldridge Cleaver, *Soul on Ice* (New York: McGraw-Hill, 1967) 14-17, 16.

P.18.   Ernest Porterfield, *Black and White Mixed Marriages* (Chicago: Nelson-Hall, 1978) 29.

P.18.   Calvin Hernton, *Sex and Racism in America* (New York: Doubleday, 1965) 119.

P.19.   Porterfield, *Black and White Mixed Marriages*, 127, 132; Lloyd Saxton, *The Individual, Marriage and the Family* (New York: Thomas Y. Crowell, 1969) 332-333; Danny K. Davis, "Sister Debates a Brother on that Black Man, White Woman

Thing," *Ebony*, August, 1970, 130-133.

P.20.    *Newsweek*, January 23, 1995, 46.

P.21.    Billingsley, *Climbing Jacob's Ladder*, 259.

P.22.    Robert Joseph Taylor, et.al., "Developments in Research on Black Families: A Decade Review," *Journal of Marriage and the Family* #52, (November, 1990) 1005-1007.

## *two* • America's Poster Boy for Sexual Deviancy

P.24.    *Newsweek*, January 23, 1995, 46.

P.24.    *LAT*, July 1, 1995, 30.

P.25.    *LAT*, July 1, 1995, 30.

P.25.    *L. A. Watts Times*, June 29, 1995, 1.

P.26.    *Time Magazine*, July 4, 1994, 20-21, 25.

P.26.    Harry Stein, "Simpson Case Isn't Grounds To Indict The Entire Gender,"*TV Guide*, July 9, 1994, 35.

P.26.    *LAT*, June 17, 1994, 24.

P.27.    *LAT*, November 3, 1994, B1.

P.27.    For an excellent discussion of why domestic battering transcends race, income and social class see Marchel Renise Barber, "Why Some Men Batter Women," *Ebony*, October, 1990, 54-57; and, Lettie L. Lockhart, "A Reexamination of the Effects of Race and Social Class on the Incidence of Marital Violence: A Search for Reliable Differences," *Journal of Marriage and the Family* #49, (August, 1987) 603-610.

P.28.    *Jewish Currents*, October, 1994, 23.

P.28.    *LAT, City Times*, October16, 1994, 4.

P.29.    Kim Deterline, "Double Standards in Domestic Violence Coverage," *Extra!* July/August 1994, 6.

P.29.    Susan Faludi, *Backlash: The Undeclared War Against Women* (New York: Anchor Books, 1991) 46-72.

P.30.    David G. Savage, "In the Matter of Justice Thomas," *LAT* Magazine, October 9, 1994, 24.

P.31.    *Time*, Nov. 29, 1993, 33; Oct. 11, 1993, 21; *Washington Post*, December 18, 1993, 7; *Wall Street Journal*, December 21, 1992, 10.

P.32.    *NYT*, July 10, 1994, E3; *LAT*, Nov. 17, 1994, 14; May 18,

1995, 1; July, 21, 1995, 29.

P.33.  *LAT*, June 21, 1995, 1.

P.33.  Jane Myers and Jill Abramson, *Strange Justice* (New York: Hougton-Mifflin, 1994) 215.

P.33.  *Newsweek*, November 14, 1994, 53.

P.35.  Lynn Norment, "What's Behind the Dramatic Rise in Rapes," *Ebony*, Sept. 1991, 92-95; *NYT* Magazine, June 13, 1993, 26.

P.35.  Jose Torres, *Fear and Fire* (New York: New American Library, 1989); *LAT*, February 8, C1; February 9, 1992 C1; Feb. 10, C1; February 12, C1; 1994; *NYT*, February 16, 1992, section 8, 11.

P.36.  *LAT*, March 26, 1995, C11.

P.36.  *NYT*, February 15, 1992, 34.

P.37.  Simpson, *I Want To Tell You*, 77.

P.38.  *Time*, August 12, 1991, 58; *Advocate*, September 10, 1991, 96; *People Weekly*, December 30, 1991, 94; *WSJ*, February 29, 1992, B3.

P.39.  *LAT*, September 19, 1993, 1.

P.39.  See Dave Kinkel, *The News Media's Picture of Children* (Children Now: Washington D.C., 1993).

P.39.  "Sexual Predators Can They Be Stopped," *U.S. News & World Report*, September 19, 1994, 65-76.

P.40.  *Newsweek*, November 14, 1994, 26-33.

P.40.  *Time*, November 14, 1994, 43-48.

P.40.  Joe Sharkey *Deadly Greed: The Stuart Murder Case in Boston and the 1980s in America* (New York: Prentice-Hall, 1991).

P.41.  *The Connection News*, November 19, 1994, 2.

P.41.  *USA Today*, November 30, 1994, 11.

P.42.  Simpson, *I Want To Tell You*, 77.

P.42.  *USA Today*, January 16, 1995, 1; January, 17, 1.

P.43.  *LAT*, July 1, 1995, 4; July 30, 1995, 16.

## *three* • The Tabloid Obsession

P.45.  Simpson, *I Want To Tell You*, 76.

P.45.  *Newsweek*, Aug. 29, 1994, 43-49.

P.45.    *Time*, June 27, 1994, 28-35.

P.46.    See Robert Ciro, *Don't Blame the People: How the news media use bias, distortion and censorship to manipulate public opinion* (Los Angeles: Diversity Press, 1971); Martin A. Lee and Norman Solomon, *Unreliable Sources* (New York: Lyle Stuart, 1990).

P.47.    *Star*, September 6, 1994, 36.

P.47.    *Newsweek*, August 29, 1994, 43.

P.47.    *The National Enquirer*, September 6, 1994, 36.

P.48.    *Examiner*, September 6, 1994,12.

P.48.    *Newsweek*, August 29, 1994, 46-47.

P.48.    *Jet*, July 18, 1994, 8-12.

P.49.    *Daily Trojan*, November 27, 1968, 2.

P.50.    *LAT*, October 2, 1994, 1.

P.50.    Lee and Solomon, *Unreliable Sources*, 72, 361-363; See Herbert Gans, *Deciding What's News* (New York: Vintage, 1980).

P.50.    *LAT*, August 3, 1995, D1.

P.50.    See Ben Bagdikian, *The Media Monopoly* (Boston: Beacon Press, 1990)

P.51.    *LAT*, July 1, 1995, 30.

P.53.    Simpson, *I Want To Tell You*, 69.

## *four* • The Real Menace to Society

P.55.    *LAT*, June 14, 1994, 1; June 18, 1995,1.

P.56.    Michael Solomowitz, "Always Running," in *O.J. Simpson: From Triumph to Tragedy* (Los Angeles: Larry Flynt Publications, 1994) 10.

P.56.    Bob Baker, "Stereotype That Won't Go Away," *LAT*, May 31, 1992, 1.

P.57.    *LAT*, June 8, 1995, 1.

P.57.    Kevin N. Wright, *The Great American Crime Myth* (New York: Praeger, 1985) 59.

P.58.    *LAT*, October 16, 1994, 1.

P.58.    *Time*, February 7, 1994, 52.

P.58.    *LAT*, July 23, 1994, 1; Jan. 13, 1994, 1; October 16, 1994, 1;

December 12, 1993, 1.

P.59.   *L.A. Sentinel,* March 10, 1994, 2.

P.59.   *LAT,* August 24, 1993, 1.

P.60.   Mira L. Boland, "Mainstream Hatred," *The Police Chief,* June 1, 1992, 30-31.

P.60.   Randall Sullivan, "Unreasonable Doubt," *Rolling Stone,* December 29-Jan. 12, 1995, 200.

P.60.   J.M. Mahoney, "Serial Murders," *The Omega-Journal of Death and Dying* #29, 1994, 29-45.

P.61.   *LAT,* November 29, 1994, 1; *USA Today,* November 30, 1994, 3.

P.61.   Walter L. Updegrave, "You're Safer Than You Think, " *Money* (June 1994), 119-121; Jesse Katz, "Crime Spawns Fear That Claims Victims of Its Own," *LAT,* December 21, 1993, 1.

P.62.   *LAT,* Aug. 8, 1995, 1.

P.62.   H. Bruce Wright, *Black Robes/White Justice* (New York: Lyle Stuart, 1992) 212.

P.63.   *LAT,* Nov. 17, 1994, D2.

P.63.   *LAT,* April, 22, 1995, 1; April, 23, 1995, 1.

P.64.   *LAT,* April 29, 1995, 1; April 30, 1995, 1; May 15, 1995, 1; *Newsweek,* July 3, 1995, 23-28.

P.65.   *Oakland Tribune,* July 30, 1995, 5.

P.65.   *Newsweek,* August 15, 1994, 25.

P.65.   Updegrave, "You're Safer Than You Think," *Money,* 116-121.

P.66.   Mike Davis, "The Sky Falls on Compton," *Nation,* September 19, 1994, 268.

P.67.   *USA Today,* July 23-25, 1994, 1; Ron Harris, "Drug War or Black War?" *LAT,* April 22, 1990, 1.

P.67.   Lionel McPherson, "News Media, Racism and the Drug War," *Extra!* April/May, 1992, 5.

P.67.   Douglas C. McDonald and Kenneth E. Carlson, *Sentencing in the Federal Courts: Does Race Matter?* (Washington D.C.: Department of Justice, December, 1993) 92-93.

P.67.   Steven Belenko, *et. al.,* "Criminal Justice Responses to Crack," *Journal of Research in Crime and Delinquency,* #28 (February 1991) 55-74; *USA Today,* Jan. 6, 1994, 1.

P.68.     *LAT*, May 21, 1995, 1; September 2, 1995, 22.

P.68.     Teresa Carpenter, "The Man Behind The Mask," *Esquire*, November 1994, 87.

P.68.     Robin Anderson, "How Reality Based Crime Shows Market Police Brutality," *Extra*, May/June, 1994, 15-17.

P.69.     *LAT*, Nov. 2, 1994, 1.

P.69.     *LAT*, April 30, 1992, 1; May 3, 1992, 7

P.70.     *LAT*, May 1, 1992, 1.

P.70.     Simpson, *I Want To Tell You*, 117-118.

P.71.     *LAT*, June 18, 1992, B9; Aug. 28, 1992, B1; May 2, 1992, 8.

P.72.     Solomowitz, *O.J.: From Triumph to Tragedy*, 60.

P.72.     *Sports Illustrated*, June 27, 1994, 22.

P.72.     *Daily Trojan*, December 17, 1968, 24.

P.73.     William H. Grier and Price M. Cobbs, *Black Rage* (New York: Bantam Books, 1968) 46-62.

P.73.     Harold M. Rose, *Race, Place and Risk: Black Homicide in Urban America*,(Albany:State University of New York Press, 1990)

P.74.     *LAT*, April 23, 1990, 1; June 10, 1992, 1.

P.74.     See Emile Durkheim, *The Rules of the Sociological Method* (New York: Free Press, 1950) 1-2, 22; Robert Nisbet and Robert G. Perrin, *The Social Bond*, 2nd. Edition (New York: Knopf, 1977) 238-239.

P.74.     William Oliver, "Black Males and the Tough Guy Image: A Dysfunctional Compensatory Adaptation," *Western Journal of Black Studies*, #8 (1984) 199.

P.75.     Roger Abrahams, *Deep Down in the Jungle: Negro Narrative Folklore from the Streets of Philadelphia* (Chicago: Aldine Co., 1970) 162-163.

P.75.     Lawrence Levine, *Black Culture and Black Consciousness* (New York: Oxford University Press, 1971) 408, 413.

P.75.     Ralph Ellison, *Invisible Man* (New York: Random House, 1982) 368.

P.76.     *Newsweek*, August 29, 1994, 44.

P.76.     *Daily Trojan*, December 17, 1968, 26

P.76.     Wright, *Native Son*, 39.

P.77.     Kirk A. Johnson, "Objective News and Other Myths: The Poisoning of Young Black Minds," *Journal of Negro Education*, #60 (1991) 333-336.

P.77.  John Langone, *The Causes of Violence* (Boston: Little Brown & Co., 1984) 49-51.

P.77.  Marshall McLuhan, *Understanding the Media* (New York: New American Library, 1964).

P.77.  National Commission on the Causes and Prevention of Violence,*Violence and the Media* (Washington D.C.: GPO, 1969) 251-252.

P.77.  *Daily Trojan*, December 17, 1968, 24.

P.77.  Kenneth Clark, *Dark Ghetto: Dilemmas of Social Power* (New York: Harper & Row, 1965) 12.

P.77.  Dick Belsky, *The Juice* (New York: David McKay, 1977) 11.

P.77.  Ronald L. Simons, *et. al.*, "Perceived Blocked Opportunity As An Explanation of Delinquency Among Lower-Class Black Males: A Research Note," *Journal of Research in Crime and Delinquency*, #26 (February 2, 1989) 90-101.

P.77.  Ulf Hannerz, "What Ghetto Males are Like: Another Look," in *Afro-American Anthropology* (New York: Free Press, 1970) 313-327.

P.77.  John Dollard, *Children of Bondage* (New York: Oxford University Press, 1939).

P.78.  Wright, *Native Son*, 39.

P.79.  Robert Chrisman and Robert L. Allen, *Court of Appeal: The Black Community Speaks Out on the Racial and Sexual Politics of Thomas vs. Hill* (New York: Ballantine, 1992) 292.

P.79.  *Final Call*, August 17, 1994, 20.

P.79.  *WSJ*, August 7, 1992, 4.

P.79.  William Oliver, "Sexual Conquest and Patterns of Black-on-Black Violence: A Statistical-Cultural Perspective", *Violence and Victims*, #4 (1989) 263-264.

P.79.  *NYT*, May 5, 1989, 11.

P.81.  *Daily Trojan,* December 17, 1968, 24.

P.81.  *Detroit Free Press*, Nov. 12, 1994, 6.

P.81.  *Newsweek*, August 29, 1994, 46.

## *five* • The Hunt for Hidden Racism

P.83.  *Daily Trojan*, October 6, 1967, 4.

P.83.    *Sports Illustrated*, June 27, 1994, 20.

P.84.    *Newsweek*, August 29, 1994, 44.

P.84.    *Daily Trojan*, January 1, 1968, 12.

P.84.    *Santa Barbara News Press*, July 24, 1994, B4.

P.85.    *Time*, August 1, 1994, 24-26.

P.85.    *LAT*, November 21, 1994, 13; February 6, 1991, 1; January 21, 1992, 1.

P.85.    *Black Enterprise*, August, 1995, 50.

P.86.    Thomas Pettigrew, "New Patterns of Racism," *Rutgers Law Review* #37 (Summer 1985) 687-691.

P.86.    *LAT*, April 30, 1995, 1; NYT, April 30, 1995, 1.

P.87.    *Time*, May 8, 1995, 44-69.

P.89.    *LAT*, November 12, 1994, 29.

P.89.    "Whites' Myths About Blacks," *U.S. News & World Report*, November 9, 1992, 47.

P.90.    Joleen Kirschman and Kathryn M. Neckerman, "We'd Love to Hire Them, But..., The Meaning of Race for Employers," in Fred L. Pincus and Howard J. Ehrlich, *Race and Ethnic Conflict* (Boulder, Co.: Westview Press, 1994) 115-124.

P.90.    "Whites' Myths....," *U.S. News & World Report*, 46.

P.90.    *Jet*, July 5, 1993, 26-28.

P.91.    Alexander Cockburn, "Double, Double Your Standard," *Extra!*, September/October, 1994, 20-21.

P.91.    *LAT*, May 2, 1992, 10.

P.91.    Charles L. Murray, "The Coming White Underclass," *WSJ*, October 29, 1993, 12.

P.91.    "Whites' Myths...," 48.

P.92.    Simpson, *I Want To Tell You*, 178.

P.92.    Charles Murray and Richard Herrnstein, *The Bell Curve* (New York: Free Press, 1994).

P.92.    Jeffrey M. Blum, *Pseudoscience and Mental Ability: The Origins and Fallacies of the IQ Controversy* (New York: Monthly Review Press, 1978) 95-96, 93-94.

P.93.    Blum,104, 77-81; Stanley Krippner, "Race, Intelligence, and Segregation: The Misuse of Scientific Data" in *White Racism*, 452-467.

P.94.   *Daily Trojan*, January 1, 1968, 12.
P.95.   *L.A. Sentinel*, August 4, 1994, 1.
P.97.   Simpson, *I Want To Tell You*, 122.


## *six* • Conspiracy *or* Collective Paranoia?

P.99.   *Final Call*, July 20, 1994, 2.
P.100.  *Newsweek*, August 1, 1994, 20.
P.100.  Joe Klein, "Can Colin Powell Save America?" *Newsweek*, October 10, 1994, 26.
P.100.  *LAT*, February 17, 1991, 8.
P.102.  *Malcolm X Speaks* (New York: Grove Press, 1965) 24.
P.103.  *Jet*, July 25, 1994, 16-18.
P.103.  *NYT*, August 11, 1991, IV, 5.
P.103.  See James H. Jones, *Bad Blood: The Tuskeegee Syphillis Experiment* (New York: Free Press, 1983).
P.105.  *Newsweek*, August 1, 1994, 19-20.
P.106.  Wright, *Native Son*, 320-321.
P.107.  *Golf Magazine*, December 1990, 52.
P.107.  See Richard Hofstadter, *The Paranoid Style in American Politics* (New York: Knopf, 1965) 6; Matthew Cooper, "The Return of the Paranoid Style in American Politics," *U.S. News & World Report*, March 12, 1990 30-31.
P.107.  *Malcolm X Speaks*, 30.
P.107.  Stephen G. Tompkins, "U.S. openly feared, secretly watched King," *Memphis Commercial Appeal*, March 21, 1993, 1; Kenneth O'Reilly, *"Racial Matters," The FBI's Secret File on Black America, 1960-1972* (New York: Free Press, 1989); Claybourne Carson, *Malcolm X: The FBI File* (New York: Carroll & Graf, 1993) 269-287, 465-484; Michael Friedly and David Gallen, *Martin Luther King-FBI File* (New York: Carroll & Graf, 1993).
P.108.  Simpson, *I Want To Tell You*, 86.
P.109.  *LAT*, July 25, 1995, C3.
P.110.  Mary A. Fischer, "The Witch Hunt, The Feds War Against Black Politicians," *Gentleman's Quarterly*, December, 1993,

244
P.111.   Mark Gladstone and Paul Jacobs, "The G-Man, the Shrimp Scam, and Sacramento's Big Story," *LAT* Magazine, December 11, 1994, 30.
P.112.   *Black Enterprise*, August 1994, 28.
P.112.   *WSJ*, May 6, 1994, C1.
P.113.   *Euromoney*, May, 1994, 24.
P.113.   *The Financial Times*, July 4, 1994, 21.

## *seven* • Delusion of the Sports Icon

P.115.   *Readers Digest*, May 1988, 30.
P.116.   Willie Mays, *Say Hey: The Autobiography of Willie Mays* (New York: Simon & Schuster, 1988) 263-265.
P.116.   *NYT*, January 11, 1991, 23; February 4, 1991, C4; March 3, 1991, VIII, 6.
P.116.   Arthur Ashe, *Days of Grace* (New York: Knopf, 1993) 126, 149, 172-173.
P.116.   Mays, *Say Hey*, 191.
P.118.   *Daily Trojan*, January 1, 1968, 12.
P.119.   *Newsweek*, August 29, 1994, 44.
P.119.   Mays, *Say Hey*, 29.
P.120.   *Time*, June 27, 1994, 32.
P.120.   *O.J.: From Triumph to Tragedy*, 31.
P.120.   *Sports Illustrated*, June 27, 1994, 27.
P.121.   Randall Sullivan, "Unreasonable Doubt," *Rolling Stone*, December 29, 1994-January 12, 1995, 146.
P.121.   *Daily Trojan*, December 12, 1967, 8.
P.121.   Leroy D. Clark, "Is It Time To Change the Playing Field?" *Emerge*, October, 1994, 59, 56.
P.122.   *Time*, June 27, 1994, 32.
P.123.   Harry Edwards, *The Revolt of the Black Athlete* (New York: Free Press, 1970).
P.123.   Jimmie Briggs, "No Defense," *Emerge*, October 1994, 52.
P.123.   *WP*, August 14, 1994, 1.
P.124.   Briggs, "No Defense," 52.

P.124.   *LAT*, May 28, 1989, VI, 6; NYT, December 14, 1991, 36.

P.125.   *Daily Trojan*, Dec. 17, 1968, 15.

P.125.   Teresa Carpenter, "The Man Behind The Mask," *Esquire*, November 1994, 88.

P.125.   Briggs, "No Defense," 53.

P.126.   Thomas Carlyle, *On Heroes and Hero Worship* (London: Oxford University Press, 1840) 12, 77.

P.126.   Paul Hoch, *Rip Off the Big Game* (New York: Doubleday, 1972) 154.

P.127.   Myriam Miedzian quoted in Robert Lipsyte, "The O.J. Syndrome," *American Health*, Sept. 1994, 50.

P.127.   *Pocket Guide to O.J. Simpson's Records*, (New York: International Collector's Society, 1994).

P.127.   *Los Angeles Bay Observer*, August 3, 1995, 8.

P.127.   *NYT*, July 1, 1994, 1.

P.127.   Janet C. Harris and Robert J. Park, "Play Game & Sports in Cultural Contexts," in *Human Kinetics* (Champaign, Ill: Publisher Inc., 1983) 107-122.

P.128.   *Time*, June 27, 1994, 32.

P.128.   E.M. Swift, "Reach Out and Touch Someone," *Sports Illustrated*, August 15, 1991, 54-58.

P.128.   *LAT*, November 3, 1994, C3.

P.129.   *LAT*, June 2, 1993, C2; *LAT*, June 8, 1993, C1.

P.129.   Ervin "Magic" Johnson with William Novak, *My Life* (New York: Random House, 1992) 249-268; *LAT*, November 9, 1991, C6.

P.130.   *LAT*, November 14, 1991, D1.

P.130.   *LAT*, December 28, 1991, D1.

P.130.   *Sports Illustrated*, June 27, 1994, 31.

P.131.   *LAT*, June 15, 1994, 18.

P.131.   *USA Today*, December13, 1994, 4.

P.132.   Belsky, *The Juice*, 27.

P.132.   Jackie Robinson, *I Never Had It Made* (New York: G. P. Putnam, 1972) 287.

## *eight* • Playing the Race Card

P.133.   *Golf Magazine*, December 1990, 53.

P.134. *USA Today*, July, 29, 1991, 1.

P.134. *WSJ*, September 29, 1994, 1.

P.135. Bob Temmey, "O.J.'s Roots," *Globe*, October 25, 1994, 23-24, 32-35.

P.135. *Newsweek*, Aug. 1, 1994, 1.

P.136. *WSJ*, August 10, 1993, 1.

P.136. Andrew Hacker, *Two Nations: Separate and Unequal* (New York: Scribners, 1992) 31-49.

P.137. *LAT*, June 4, 1995, M3.

P.137. *WSJ*, October 24, 1994, 14; *The Connection*, November 19, 1994, 4.

P.138. Tom Raum, "General Colin Powell May Be the Eisenhower of the 90s'," *L.A. Sentinel*, September 29, 1994,14.

P.138 *LAT*, September 17, 1995.

P.138. Klein, "Can Colin Powell Save America?" 18-26.

P.138. *Newsweek*, Aug. 29, 1994, 46.

P.140. Joe R. Feagin and Melvin P. Sikes, *Living With Racism: The Black Middle-Class Experience* (Boston: Beacon Press, 1994) 29-33, 38-47, 47-56.

P.140. Feagin, "The Continuing Significance of Race: Antiblack Discrimination in Public Places," *American Sociological Review*, #56 (Feb. 1991) 101-116.

P.141. *New York Beacon*, December 10-December 16, 1994, 4.

P.141. *LAT*, July 28, 1991, 1.

P.141. *LAT*, November 5, 1991, 1.

P.142. *Newsweek*, Aug.29, 1994, 45.

P.143. *LAT*, March 20, 1995, 19.

P.143. Peter Brimelow and Leslie Spencer, "When Quotas Replace Merit, Everybody Suffers," *Forbes*, February 15, 1993, 80-102.

P.143. Andrea H. Butler, "The Economics of Enforcement of the Antidiscrimination Law: Title VII of the Civil Rights Act of 1964," *Journal of Law and Economics* #21 (Oct. 1978) 359-380.

P.144. Fred L. Pincus, "The Case for Affirmative Action," in Pincus and Erhlich, *Race and Ethnic Conflict* (Boulder, Co.: Westview Press, 1994) 368-378.

P.144. Ellis Cose, "To The Victors Few Spoils," *Newsweek*, March 29, 1993, 54

P.144. *WSJ*, September 14, 1993, 1.

P.144.   George Davis and Clegg Watson, *Black Life in Corporate America* (New York: Anchor Books, 1982) 166-186.

P.144.   Feagin and Sikes, *Living With Racism*, 135-136.

P.144.   Sara Fritz, "More and More Workers Falling Victim to Companies Downsizing," *LAT*, December 25, 1992, 4.

P.146.   David Treadwell, "Hard Road for Black Business, " *LAT*, September 20, 1991, 1.

P.147.   Fusfield, "The Political Economy of the Urban Ghetto," 12-36

P.147.   *Black Enterprise*, August 1995, 50.

P.147.   Feagin and Sikes, *Living With Racism*, 203.

P.148.   James E. Ellis, "The Black Middle Class," *Business Week*, March 14, 1988, 64.

P.148.   Douglass S. Massey, "Residential Segregation in American Cities" in *Race and Ethnic Conflict in America*, 126-127.

P.148.   Feagin and Sikes, *Living With Racism*, 223-272, 228, 264.

P.149.   *LAT*, January 14, 1995, 179.

P.149.   Simpson, *I Want To Tell You*, 112-113.

P.150.   Massey and Mitchell L. Eggers, "The Ecology of Inequality: Minorities and the Concentration of Poverty, 1970-1980," *American Journal of Sociology*, #95 (March, 1990) 1186.

P.150.   Richard Lacayo, "Between Two Worlds," *Time*, March 13, 1989, 58-68.

P.151.   *Newsweek*, August 29, 1994, 45.

P.151.   *Golf Magazine*, December 1990, 53.

## *nine* • Justice for Sale

P.153.   *LAT*, July 9, 1994, 1.

P.153.   *LAT*, July 1, 1994, 1.

P.154.   Stephen B. Bright, "Counsel for the Poor: The Death Sentence Not For the Worst Crime but for the Worst Lawyer," *Yale Law Journal*, #103 (May, 1994) 1846.

P.155.   *Forbes*, August 29, 1994, 18.

P.155.   Bright, "Counsel for the Poor," 1844-1845.

P.156.   David L. Bazelon, "The Defective Assistance of Counsel,"

*University of Cincinnati Law Review* #42 (1973) 26.

P.156.     Thomas M. Ross, "Rights at the Ballot Box: The Effect of Judicial Elections on Judge's Ability to Protect Criminal Defendant's Rights," *Law & Inequality*, #7 (1988) 107.

P.156.     *LAT*, July 20, 1994, 1.

P.157.     *LAT*, Sept. 10, 1994, 1; Sept. 11, 1994, 1.

P.158.     *LAT*, Oct. 27, 1994, 1.

P.159.     *LAT*, Aug. 11, 1994, 3.

P.159.     *LAT*, Oct. 22, 1994, 26.

P.159.     *Newsweek*, Aug. 22, 1994 29.

P.159.     *LAT*, Sept. 28, 1994, 16.

P.160.     Dierde Golash, "Jury Selection," *Behavioral Sciences and the Law*, #10 (Spring 1992) 162.

P.160.     Elizabeth L. Earle, "Banishing the Thirteenth Juror: An Approach to the Identification of Prosecutorial Racism," *Columbia Law Review*, #92 (June 1992) 1217.

P.160.     *LAT*, September 25, 1994, 22.

P.160.     Charles R. Lawrence, "The Id, the Ego and Equal Protection: Reckoning with Unconscious Racism," *Stanford Law Review*, #39 (1987) 317-325.

P.160.     Lynn Kessler, "The Trial in Simi Valley," Research Paper, Private Copy in Author's Possession, 8-9.

P.160.     George S. Bridges and Robert D. Crutchfield, "Law, Social Standing and Racial Disparities in Imprisonment," *Social Forces*, # 66 (March, 1988) 699-720; Charles W. Peek, et.al.,"Race and AttitudesToward Local police: Another Look," *Journal of Black Studies*, #2 (March, 1981) 361-374.

P.161.     *LAT*, September 25, 1994, 3.

P.162.     *LAT*, November 3, 1994, B1.

P.162.     Hiroshi Fukari, *et. al.*,"Where Did All the Black Jurors Go?" *Journal of Black Studies*, #22 (Dec. 1991) 196-215.

P.162.     Jeffrey Sobal, "Bias Against Marginal Individuals in a Jury Wheel Selection," *Journal of Criminal Justice*, #14 (1986) 71-89.

P.162.     *LAT*, June 2, 1994, 1.

P.162.     *LAT*, Sept. 24, 1994, 22.

P.162.     *L.A. Sentinel*, Nov. 10, 1994, 4.

P.162.     *LAT*, Oct. 28, 1994, 1; Nov. 4, 1994, 1; Nov. 5, 1994, 1.

P.162. Deborah Denno, "Psychological Factors for the Black Defendant in a Jury Trial," *Journal of Black Studies*, #22 (March, 1981) 313-326.

P.162. Michael Knox, *The Diary of An Ex-O.J. Juror* (Los Angeles: Dove Books, 1995); *LAT*, June 25, 1995, B1.

P.163. *Newsweek*, April 17, 1995, 26-28.

P.163. *LAT*, July 25, 1995, 12; *L.A. Watts Times*, June 29, 1995, 1.

P.164. *L.A. Watts Times*, June 29, 1995, 1.

P.165. *LAT*, June 14, 1995, 1.

P.166. *L.A. Watts Times*, June 29, 1995, 1.

P.167. "Whites' Myths About Blacks," *U.S. News & World Report*, 47.

P.167. *LAT*, April 6, 1995, 1.

P.168. *LAT*, Nov. 15, 1994, 1.

P.168. *LAT*, Sept. 28, 1994, 16; Sept. 28, 1994, 1.

P.169. Richard Seltzer, et. al., "Juror Honesty During *Voir Dire*," *Journal of Criminal Justice*, #19 (1991) 451-462.

P.170. Steven D. DeBrotz, "Arguments Appealing to Racial Prejudice," *Indiana Law Journal*, #64 (Spring 1989) 376-377.

P.170. Earle, "Prosecutorial Racism," 1225, 1231.

P.170. Michael A. Jeter, "Case Note, Criminal Law—The Right to an Impartial trial is protected by an opportunity to Prove that Juror Bias or Prosecutorial misconduct Affected the outcome of the Trial," *Howard Law Journal*, #26 (1983) 799, 803.

P.170. Earle, "Prosecutorial Racism," 1224-1225.

P.171. Simpson, *I Want To Tell You*, 91.

P.173. *LAT*, June 4, 1990, 33; June 25, 1991, 5.

P.173. Bright, "Counsel for the Poor," 1858, 1849.

P.174. Peter Appelbome, "Study Fault's Atlanta's System of Defending Poor," *NYT*, November 30, 1990, B5.

P.175. *WP*, Sept. 11, 1992, 6.

P.176. *American Lawyer*, January/February 1993, 46.

P.176. Paul C. Drecksel, "The Crisis in Indigent Criminal Defense," *Arkansas Law Review*, #44(1991) 363-390

P.176. *LAT*, June 11, 1994, 1.

P.176. Richard Klein, "The Eleventh Commandment: Thou Shall Not be Compelled to Render Ineffective Assistance of

Counsel," *Indiana Law Journal,* #68 (1993) 370.

P.176.    Edward C. Monahan, "Who Is Trying to Kill the Sixth Amendment?" *ABA Criminal Justice,* (Summer, 1991) 24-28.

P.177.    Bright, "Counsel for the Poor," 1856.

## *Conclusion* • *Race, Sex, and Class Lessons for America*

P.179.    *Culver City Independent,* September 29, 1994, 1.

# Bibliography

Ashe, Arthur. *Days of Grace* (New York: Knopf, 1993).

Bagdikian, Ben. *The Media Monopoly* (Boston: Beacon Press, 1990).

Belsky, Dick. *The Juice* (New York: David McKay, 1977).

Billingsley, Andrew. *Climbing Jacob's Ladder: The Enduring Legacy of African-American Families* (New York: Simon & Schuster, 1992).

Blum, Jeffrey M. *Pseudoscience and Mental Ability: The Origins and Fallacies of the IQ Controversy* (New York: Monthly Review Press, 1978).

Carson, Claybourne. *Malcolm X: The FBI File* (New York: Carroll & Graf, 1993).

Chrisman, Robert and Allen, Robert L. *Court of Appeal: The Black Community Speaks Out on the Racial and Sexual Politics of Thomas vs. Hill* (New York: Ballantine, 1992).

Cose, Ellis. *The Rage of a Privileged Class* (New York: Harper-Collins, 1993).

Edwards, Harry. *The Revolt of the Black Athlete* (New York: Free Press, 1970).

Ellison, Ralph. *Invisible Man* (New York: Random House, 1982).

Faludi, Susan. *Backlash: The Undeclared War Against Women* (New York: Anchor Books, 1991).

Feagin, Joe R. and Sykes, Melvin P. *Living With Racism: The Black Middle-Class Experience* (Boston: Beacon Press, 1994).

Flowers, Ronald Barri. *Minorities and Criminality* (New York: Greenwood Press, 1990).

Frederickson, George M. *The Black Image in the White Mind* (New York: Harper & Row, 1971).

Friedly, Michael and Gallen, David. *Martin Luther King, Jr: The FBI File* (New York: Carroll & Graf, 1993).

Fusfield, Daniel. *The Political Economy of the Urban Ghetto* (Carbondale, Ill.: Southern Illinois University Press, 1982).

Gilmore, Al-Tony. *Bad Nigger! The National Impact of Jack Johnson* (Port Washington, NY: Kennikat Press, 1975).

Gossett, Thomas F. *Race: The History of an Idea in America* (New York: Schocken Books, 1965).

Grier, William H. and Cobbs, Price M. *Black Rage* (New York: Bantam Books, 1968).

Hernton, Calvin. *Sex and Racism in America* (New York: Doubleday, 1965).

Hoch, Paul. *Rip Off The Big Game* (New York: Doubleday, 1972).

Hofstadter, Richard. *The Paranoid Style in American Politics* (New York: Knopf, 1965).

Jenkins, James. *The Politics of Empowerment* (Detroit: Wayne State University, 1992).

Kluger, Richard. *Simple Justice* (New York: Knopf, 1976).

Levine, Lawrence. *Black Culture and Black Consciousness* (New York: Oxford University Press, 1971).

Langone, John. *The Causes of Violence* (Boston: Little, Brown & Co., 1984).

Lee, Martin and Solomon, Norman. *Unreliable Sources* (New York: Lyle Stuart, 1990).

Logan, Rayford W. *The Betrayal of the Negro* (New York: Harper & Row, 1962).

McDonald, Douglas C. and Carlson Kenneth E. *Sentencing in the Federal Courts: Does Race Matter?* (Washington D.C.: Department of Justice, December, 1993).

Mann, Coramae Richey. *Unequal Justice: A Question of Color* (Bloomington, Ind.: Indiana University Press, 1993).

Mathabane, Mark and Mathabane, Gail. *Black and White: The Triumph of Love over Prejudice and Taboo* (New York: Harper & Collins, 1992).

Mays, Willie. *Say Hey: The Autobiography of Willie Mays* (New York: Simon & Schuster, 1988).

Murray, Charles and Herrnstein, Richard. *The Bell Curve* (New York: Free Press, 1994).

*O.J.: From Triumph to Tragedy* (Beverly Hills, Ca.: Larry Flynt Publications, 1994).

Pincus, Fred L. and Ehrlich, Howard J. *Race and Ethnic Conflict* (Boulder: Westview Press, 1994).

Porterfield, Ernest. *Black and White Mixed Marriage* (Chicago: Nelson-Hall, 1978).

O'Reilly, Kenneth *"Racial Matters" The FBI's Secret File on Black America, 1960-1972* (New York: Free Press, 1989).

Rose, Harold M. *Race, Place and Risk: Black Homicide in Urban America* (Albany: SUNY Press, 1990).

Simpson, O.J. *I Want To Tell You* (Boston: Little, Brown & Co., 1995).

Wright, Kevin N. *The Great American Crime Myth* (New York: Praeger, 1985).

Wright, Richard. *Native Son* (New York: Harper & Row, 1966).

# Index

## W

## INDIGNANT HEART

*A Black Worker's Journal*
**Charles Denby**

A two-part account of a U.S. activist's battle for freedom, first personally and then as a supporter of the principal movements of the last twenty-five years.

**295 pages**
**Paperback ISBN: 0-919618-67-7**            **$9.99**
**Hardcover ISBN: 0-919618-93-6**            **$38.99**


## BETWEEN THE LINES

*How to Detect Bias and Propaganda in the News and Everyday Life*
**Eleanor MacLean**

*Taking professional journalism to task for not practising fully enough the lofty ideals it preaches.*
**Canadian Journal of Communication**
*An excellent resource tool for teachers.*
**Kingston Whig-Standard**

**296 pages**
**Paperback ISBN: 0-919619-12-6**            **$19.99**
**Hardcover ISBN: 0-919619-14-2**            **$48.99**


## BEYOND HYPOCRISY

*Decoding the News in an Age of Propaganda*
Including a Doublespeak Dictionary for the 1990s

### Edward S. Herman

Illustrations by Matt Wuerker

In a highly original volume that includes an extended essay on the Orwellian use of language that characterizes U.S. political culture, cartoons, and a cross-referenced lexicon of *doublespeak* terms with examples of their all too frequent usage, Herman and Wuerker highlight the deception and hypocrisy contained in the U.S. government's favourite buzz-words.

*Rich in irony and relentlessly forthright, Beyond Hypocrisy is a valuable resource for those interested in avoiding... 'an unending series of victories over your own memory'.*
**Montréal Mirror**
*Edward Herman starts out with a good idea and offers a hard-hitting and often telling critique of American public life.*
**Ottawa Citizen**

**239 pages, illustrations, index**
**Paperback ISBN: 1-895431-48-4**      **$19.99**
**Hardcover ISBN: 1-895431-49-2**      **$48.99**

## A PASSION FOR RADIO

### *Radio Waves and Community*
### Bruce Girard, ed.

A project of the World Association of Community Radio Broadcasters, this book tells the stories of alternative radio projects around the globe—stories about a passion for fundamental social change, in a great diversity of situations from First Nations in the Canadian North, to punks in Amsterdam, progressives in California, guerrillas in El Salvador, genuine revolutionaries in ex-Communist countries.

*The stories in this book are moving and inspiring.*
**Media Development**
*Some will find the stories disturbing, but all will learn of the power of the medium.*
**Monitoring Times**
*This impressive book is an exciting window into the increasingly diffuse world of participatory media.*
**Media Information Australia**

**212 pages**
**Paperback ISBN: 1-895431-34-4**      **$19.99**
**Hardcover ISBN: 1-895431-35-2**      **$48.99**
**L.C. No. 91-72979**

## COMMON CENTS

### *Media Portrayal of the Gulf War and Other Events*
### James Winter

Objectivity is the theme of these five case studies which deal with how the media covered the Gulf War, the Oka standoff, the Ontario NDP's budget, the Meech Lake Accord and Free Trade. Winter shows how media coverage of events consistently casts them in what becomes a seemingly apolitical 'common-sense' framework, a framework which actually represents the opinions of the power elite.

*Like Chomsky, he enjoys contrasting the "common-sense" interpretation with views from alternative sources. As facts and images clash, we end up with a better grasp of the issues at hand.*
**Montréal Gazette**

*Winter's analysis of why the media fail to tell us all, in greater, more useful depth, gives us some basis for hope and perhaps humor.*
**Peace Magazine**

**304 pages, index**
**Paperback ISBN: 1-895431-24-7**               **$23.99**
**Hardcover ISBN: 1-895431-25-5**               **$52.99**
**L.C. No. 92-70624**

## ELECTRIC RIVERS
### *The Story of the James Bay Project*
### Sean McCutcheon

*... a book about how and why the James Bay project is being built, how it works, the consequences its building will have for people and for the environment... it cuts through the rhetoric so frequently found in the debate.*
**Canadian Book Review Annual**
*Electric Rivers is a welcome contribution to the debate... a good fortune for readers who would like to better understand a story that is destined to dominate the environmental and political agenda.*
**Globe and Mail**

**194 pages, maps**
**Paperback ISBN: 1-895431-18-2**               **$18.99**
**Hardcover ISBN: 1-895431-19-0**               **$47.99**
**L.C. No. 91-72981**

## BATTERED WOMEN
### Micheline Beaudry

*An excellent study of policies affecting the women's shelter movement.*
**Quill & Quire**

**118 pages, appendices**
**Paperback ISBN: 0-920057-46-2**               **$12.99**
**Hardcover ISBN: 0-920057-47-0**               **$41.99**

## THE DECLINE OF THE AMERICAN ECONOMY
### Bertrand Bellon and Jorge Niosi

translated by Robert Chodos and Ellen Garmaise

Two prominent economists examine the decline of U.S. industry, covering the post-World War period to the Reagan era.

*A convenient summary of a vast amount of research... packed with facts and figures.*
**The Village Voice**

**242 pages, index, bibliography**
**Paperback ISBN: 0-921689-00-4**               **$16.99**
**Hardcover ISBN: 0-921689-01-2**               **$45.99**

# RACE, GENDER AND WORK

## *A Multi-Cultural Economic History of Women in the United States*
## Teresa Amott and Julie Matthaei

Race, Gender, and Work *is exciting because of its frank acknowledgement of difference among women. It is a volume that will inform and motivate scholars and activists.*
**Julianne Malveaux, University of California, Berkeley**
... *a detailed, richly textured history of American working women.*
**Barbara Ehrenreich, author of The Worst Years of Our Lives**

**433 pages, index, appendices**
**Paperback ISBN: 0-921689-90-X**        **$19.99**
**Hardcover ISBN: 0-921689-91-8**        **$48.99**

# FRIENDLY FASCISM

## *The New Face of Power in America*
## Bertram Gross

A provocative and original study of current trends in the U.S. resulting in a forecast of totalitarianism.

*Gross leaves the reader breathless. Friendly Fascism is historical and journalistic.*
**Fuse Magazine**

**410 pages, index**
**Paperback ISBN: 0-920057-23-3**        **$19.99**
**Hardcover ISBN: 0-920057-22-5**        **$48.99**

# IMAGINING THE MIDDLE EAST

## Thierry Hentsch

translated by Fred A. Reed

### *Recipient of the Governor General's Literary Award for Translation*

*For readers who want to understand the world of plural identities and the tactics of "appropriation," this is a very rich and necessary book.*
**Montréal Gazette**
*This Canadian professor adds to the critique of Orientalism... a stimulating work.*
**Journal of Palestine Studies**
*This remarkable book... could be seen as advancing our understanding beyond professor Edward Said's Orientalism.*
**Crescent**
*Fresh insights into the areas of the "mythical frontier"... a thorough and valuable account.*
**Arab Studies Quarterly**

**218 pages, index**
**Paperback ISBN: 1-895431-12-3**        **$19.99**
**Hardcover ISBN: 1-895431-13-1**        **$48.99**

# HOT MONEY AND THE POLITICS OF DEBT
## R.T. Naylor

*2nd edition*

### Introduction by Leonard Silk, former financial editor of the New York Times

A ball of hot money rolls around the world. It seeks anonymity and political refuge: it dodges taxes and sidesteps currency controls; it rolls through shell companies and numbered accounts, phoney charities and religious foundations. And as the ball of hot money grows, so, too, does the international debt crisis. For hot money and the international debt are two sides of the same devalued coin.

*As conspiracy theories go, here is one that is truly elegant. It involves everybody.*
**Washington Post**
*... a fascinating survey of international finance scams.*
**Globe and Mail**
*A startling and informative book which everyone... should read.*
**Lloyd's List**
*Naylor discusses the global pool of hot and homeless money... how it is used and abused.*
**Journal of Economic Literature**

540 pages, index
Paperback ISBN: 1-895431-94-8                    $19.99
Hardcover ISBN: 1-895431-95-6                    $48.99
L.C. No. 94-071245


# YEAR 501
## *The Conquest Continues*
## Noam Chomsky

*2nd printing*

A powerful and comprehensive discussion of the incredible injustices hidden in our history.

*... Year 501 offers a savage critique of the new world order.*
**MacLean's Magazine**
*Tough, didactic, [Chomsky] skins back the lies of those who make decisions.*
**Globe and Mail**
*... a much-needed defense against the mind-numbing free market rhetoric.*
**Latin America Connexions**

331 pages, index
Paperback ISBN: 1-895431-62-X                    $19.99
Hardcover ISBN: 1-895431-63-8                    $48.99

# RADICAL PRIORITIES
## Carlos P. Otero, ed.

*2nd revised edition, 4th printing*

*A fuller picture of Chomsky's fascinating political scholarship.*
**Harvard International Review**
*... another valuable collection of Chomsky's political and social criticism.*
**The Village Voice**
*We are indebted to the editor, C.P. Otero, for this collection.*
**The Humanist in Canada**
**307 pages**
**Paperback ISBN: 0-920057-17-9**     **$19.99**
**Hardcover ISBN: 0-920057-16-0**     **$48.99**

# JFK, the Vietnam War, and U.S. Political Culture
## Noam Chomsky

For those who turn to Hollywood for history, and confuse creative license with fact, Chomsky proffers an arresting reminder that historical narrative rarely fits neatly into a feature film.

*... a fascinating and disturbing portrait of the Kennedy dynasty.*
**Briarpatch**
*... a particularly interesting and important instance of media and power elite manipulation.*
**Humanist In Canada**
*... the most important contribution to the ongoing public and private discussions about JFK.*
**Kitchener-Waterloo Record**
**172 pages, index**
**Paperback ISBN: 1-895431-72-7**     **$19.99**
**Hardcover ISBN: 1-895431-73-5**     **$48.99**

# THE ECOLOGY OF FREEDOM
## *The Emergence and Dissolution of Hierarchy, revised edition*
## Murray Bookchin

*The most systematic articulation of ideas.*
**San Francisco Review of Books**
*... a confirmation of his [Bookchin's] status as a penetrating critic not only of the ways in which humankind is destroying itself, but of the ethical imperative to live better.*
**The Village Voice**
*Elegantly written, and recommended for a wide audience.*
**Library Journal**

**395 pages, index, L.C. No. 90-83628**
**Paperback ISBN: 0-921689-72-1**     **$19.99**
**Hardcover ISBN: 0-921689-73-X**     **$48.99**

# MANUFACTURING CONSENT

## *Noam Chomsky And the Media*
## Mark Achbar, ed.

*2nd printing*

*Manufacturing Consent Noam Chomsky and the Media*, the companion book to the award-winning film, charts the life of America's most famous dissident, from his boyhood days running his uncle's newsstand in Manhattan to his current role as outspoken social critic.

*A juicily subversive biographical/philosophical documentary bristling and buzzing with ideas.*
**Washington Post**
*You will see the whole sweep of the most challenging critic in modern political thought.*
**Boston Globe**
*One of our real geniuses... an excellent introduction.*
**Village Voice**
*An intellectually challenging crash course in the man's cooly contentious analysis, laying out his thoughts in a package that is clever and accessible.*
**Los Angeles Times**
*... challenging, controversial... the unravelling of ideas.*
**Globe and Mail**
*...lucid and coherent statement of Chomsky's thesis.*
**The Times of London**
*... invaluable as a record of a thinker's progress towards basic truth and basic decency.*
**The Guardian**

**264 pages, 270 illustrations, bibliography, index**
**Paperback ISBN: 1-551640-02-3      $19.99**
**Hardcover ISBN: 1-551640-03-1      $48.99**

# FEMINISM

## Angela Miles and Geraldine Finn, eds.

*2nd revised edition*

*A positive sign that feminism continues to be a healthy, growing movement that is joyfully redefining what it means to be fully human.*
**United Church Observer**
*... a very satisfying book... highly readable, well-argued, stimulating, and provocative... provides an alternative feminist framework to guide how scholarship and politics should be carried out.*
**Canadian Journal of Political Science**

**400 pages, bibliography**
**Paperback ISBN: 0-921689-22-5   $19.99**
**Hardcover ISBN: 0-921689-23-3   $48.99**

# BLACK ROSE BOOKS

*has also published the following books of related interest*

Democracy's Oxygen: How the News Media Smother the Facts,
   *by James Winter*
Perspectives on Power: Reflections on Human Nature and the Social
   Order, *by Noam Chomsky*
Into the European Mirror: The Works of Julian Samuel, *edited by*
   *Aruna Handa and John Kipphoff*
The Trojan Horse: Alberta and the Future of Canada, *edited by*
   *Gordon Laxer and Trevor Harrison*
Shelter, Housing and Homes: A Social Right, *by Arnold Bennett*
Complicity: Human Rights and Canadian Foreign Policy, *by Sharon Scharfe*
Local Places: In the Age of the Global City,
   *edited by Roger Keil, Gerda Wekerle and David Bell*
The Regulation of Desire: Homo and Hetero Sexualities, *by Gary Kinsman*
Free Trade: Neither Free Nor About Trade, *by Christopher Merrett*
The Other Mexico: The North American Triangle Completed,
   *by John Warnock*
First Person Plural: A Community Development Approach to Social
   Change, *by David Smith*
The City and Radical Social Change, *by Dimitri Roussopoulos*
Toward an Ecological Society, *Murray Bookchin*
The Philosophy of Social Ecology, *Murray Bookchin*
Nature and the Crisis of Modernity, *by Raymond A. Rogers*
Political Arrangements: Power and the City, *edited by Henri Lustiger-Thaler*
Bringing the Economy Home From the Market, *by Ross Dobson*
Balance: Art and Nature, *by John Grande*
The Anarchist Papers, *by Dimitrios Roussopoulos, ed.*
Communication: For and Against Democracy, *by Marc Raboy and Peter A.*
   *Bruck, eds.*

*send for a free catalogue of all our titles*
*BLACK ROSE BOOKS*
*P.O. Box 1258*
*Succ. Place du Parc*
*Montréal, Québec*
*H3W 2R3 Canada*
*To order books: (phone) 1-800-565-9523 (fax) 1-800-221-9985*


*Printed by the workers of*
*Les Ateliers Graphiques Marc Veilleux Inc.*
*Cap-Saint-Ignace, Québec*
*for Black Rose Books Ltd.*

«L'IMPRIMEUR»